Ishii Shiro

Josef Mengele of the East

Pacific Atrocities Education

Ishii Shiro

*Josef Mengele
of the East*

JENNY CHAN

Ishii Shiro

*Josef Mengele
of the East*

Written by
Jenny Chan

Editor
Barbara Halperin

Published by Pacific Atrocities Education

In Collaboration with
Education for Social Justice

Paperback ISBN: 978-1-947766-34-1

E-book ISBN: 978-1-947766-22-8

Table of Contents

Introduction

Ishii Shiro and Josef Mengele shown in the pictures above are very similar in many ways although they were miles apart during WWII. They both grew up on a farm, were both military scientists in the Axis of Power during WWII, made advances in biological weapons research, conducted human experimentation, and walked away after the war without any justice being served.

Born into a relatively wealthy family, Mengele's father was the founder of Karl Mengele & Sons farming machinery company. He joined the Nazi party in Munich in 1930 while studying philosophy in college and went on to studying anthropology and medicine. He used the opportunity in Auschwitz to conduct research using humans as experimental subjects, mostly focusing on heredity and pathogens. His most well-known studies were in the field of heredity in an effort to prove the superiority of the Aryan race.

Most of his victims were Jews who were forcibly transported by rail from all over German occupied Europe. Upon arrival, they were either designated as slave labor or subjects for human experimentation. Those chosen for human experimentation were treated better than the other prisoners in Auschwitz and temporarily spared from execution. Auschwitz survivors recalled Mengele as being a character who was able to charm his victims before subjecting them to the cruelest treatment. Mengele shipped organs and specimens from his research to the Germany Research Foundation and, in return, received money from the Foundation to build a pathology laboratory attached to Crematorium II at Auschwitz II-Birkenau. The laboratory, also known as the Institute for Heredity, included experiments such as transfusing blood from one twin to another, infecting subjects with diseases, and performing unnecessary amputations in the name of advancing science.

Ishii Shiro, the Nazi scientist's counterpart in Japan, had a similar journey to Josef Mengele. Coming from a landowning class, he studied medicine at Kyoto Imperial University and later was commissioned in the Imperial Japanese Army as a military surgeon. As a charming researcher, he was able to network his way up the career ladder. After Japan occupied Manchuria, he became the leader of Unit 731, a covert biological and chemical warfare research and development unit of the Imperial Japanese Army.

Money for the laboratory was provided by the Kwantung Army as Ishii had convinced his superior that using biological weapons was the most cost effective way to fight any war. In Unit 731, personnel performed human experimentation, collected specimen samples, developed biological weaponry and, subsequently, carried out biological warfare against civilians in China and Russia. Human experimentation included vivisection, intense exposure in pressure chambers, blood transfusions, deadly diseases, frostbite experiments, and unnecessary amputations. Organs were sent back to Tokyo and biological weapons or vaccines then were developed based on research results.

In terms of biological warfare, Ishii led the offensive military staff that sprayed biological weapons across China and the Soviet Union. Many of the Chinese victims were irreversibly sickened with glanders and anthrax and have suffered from rotten legs for more than 70 years after the war's end. Even if infection did not occur immediately, the population's offspring working on their land contracted diseases from bacteria that survived in the soil for years. It was not until 2014 that the victims were able to find treatment.

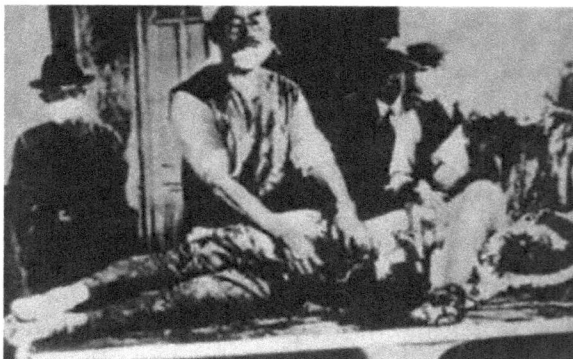

Although during WWII, Ishii Shiro was older and more established than Josef Mengele, Ishii Shiro was ranked Lieutenant-General while Josef Mengele was only a Captain, meaning that Ishii had significantly more power than his Nazi counterpart. Unit 731 was not a stand-alone entity of Ishii Shiro. At one point, if a scientist was working in the medical field in Japan, he was a part of the Ishii Network. In addition to Unit 731, there were other subsidiary plants as well, otherwise known as death factories. At the end of the war, under the order of Ishii's superior, the entire complex of Unit 731 was destroyed. As the staff and troops left, they also left behind the world's largest chemical and biological dump while Ishii Shiro traded the results of his work for immunity from the United States. Through efforts to downplay what actually took place at Unit 731 and the lack of a trial, Ishii Shiro is far less known than his Nazi counterpart, despite the fact that his research produced information still employed in modern warfare.

Chapter 1

Background: History of Biological Weapons and Japanese Ultranationalism

The use of biological weapons pre-dated WWII. Military history shows that diseases had been well used. Examples include the Anatolian War in 1320-1318 B.C., the Romans and the Persians regularly poisoning their enemies' wells, and the Mongols disposing of diseased corpses in towns they needed to conquer. In more recent military history, British and American soldiers gave Native Americans blankets contaminated with smallpox.

As the United States began westward expansion through Manifest Destiny, it showed off its power on the international stage. In 1851, Matthew Perry arrived in Japanese waters with a squadron of Navy ships authorized by President Millard Fillmore and forced Japan to open up trade with the West.[1] At the time, Japan was a feudalistic country with no advanced technology, but from trading with the United States, it found a way to industrialize even with the small amount of resources.

In order to advance its national goal of industrialization, Japan needed resources. They started territorial disputes with Manchuria and Korea. When negotiations broke down, Japan attacked Russia in Port Arthur, which led to the Russo-Japanese War. It was then that Japan realized that diseases could be as deadly as firepower. Japanese soldiers were suffering from cholera, beri-beri, typhoid fever, and diarrheal diseases and about 25,000 of the 80,000 men in the Third Army were sent during the siege of Port Arthur.[2] Japan then established its first Epidemic Prevention Laboratory.[3] By the beginning of the 20th century Japanese scientists were well known for their work in preventative medicine. Similar to their efforts toward industrialization, the Japanese scientists worked hard and discovered the cause of beri-

---

[1] "The United States and the Opening to Japan, 1853," *U.S. Department of State*, U.S. Department of State, history.state.gov/milestones/1830-1860/opening-to-japan.
[2] Hawk, Alan, "The Great Disease Enemy, Kak'ke (Beriberi) and the Imperial Japanese Army", *Military Medicine*, Volume 171, Issue 4, April 2006, p. 333-339.
[3] Gold, Hal, *Unit 731 Testimony: Japan's Wartime Human Experimentation Program*, Boston: Tuttle Publishing, 2004, p. 22.

beri and dysentery. The Shiga bacillus, a strain of bacteria which causes dysentery, was named after the Japanese scientist who discovered it.[4]

In response to the Russians poisoning wells in Manchuria with typhoid, dysentery, and cholera, the Japanese developed a portable water testing kit. In order to treat the ingestion problem during wartime, each soldier was given a creosote pill after a meal. In a short period of time, Japan made a great deal of progress in the field of preventative medicine comparable to the West.

A decade after the Russo-Japanese War, the German army's use of chemical weapons inflicted heavy civilian casualties in World War I. Consequently, on June 17, 1925, 44 countries passed an agreement at the 1925 Conference on Disarmament in Geneva and signed an international protocol named "Protocol for the Prohibition of the Use in War of Asphyxiating, Poisonous or other Gases, and of Bacteriological Methods of Warfare" ("Geneva Protocol"). The agreement prohibited the use of chemical and biological weapons in war. Representatives from Japan were also present at this conference and were involved in drafting and signing the Geneva Protocol (although it was not ratified in Japan at the time).

After WWI ended, although Japan joined the

---

[4] Ibid. p. 17.

League of Nations as the only great power in Asia, Japanese officials still felt as if the West was not treating them equally. Due to the lack of industrial needs after the war, Japan was experiencing the worst economic crisis in its history. Some described this time period in the 1920s as a chronic depression. Right after the boom of the First World War, stock prices in Japan experienced a hard landing. Later, around 1923, the Great Kanto Earthquake's physical damage resulted in huge losses. By the time the 1930s arrived, the world was experiencing a global depression. The West imposed tariffs on Japanese goods through the Smoot-Hawley Tariff Act which introduced a new sense of nationalism in Japan. As Japan experienced economic turmoil, political groups that promised to fix things became more prominent. Two of those groups were the Black Dragon Society and the Cherry Blossom Society.

The Cherry Blossom Society's membership quickly grew in size with the focus on ultra-nationalism. Members were in the military, education, and media fields. A notable figure was General Araki Sadao, appointed Army Minister in 1931, who was a strong advocate for the Kodoha policy, which was the "Imperial Way." It advocated expansionism, totalitarianism, and a greater military.[5] The Board of Infor-

---

[5] Interview with General Araki Sadao by Gareth Jones, Tokyo on November 3rd, 1935.

mation censored the media information which conflicted with the army by this time. In the same time period, education was radicalized. Scholarships no longer went to students solely for good grades or hard work, but to students who personified the Imperial Japanese Army's ideals of discipline, tradition, strength, and loyalty to the Emperor. History books were revised and dangerous thoughts from the West which contradicted the Army's ways were considered a type of crime. With the newfound ultranationalism, the Imperial Japan Army staged an incident in Manchuria to simultaneously take territory and quit the League of Nations.

The Young Ishii Shiro

In an interview in 1982 in the Japan Times, the eldest daughter of Ishii Shiro, Harumi Ishii, stated, "Were it not for the war and his chosen career, his genius might have flourished in a field other than medical science, possibly, politics." She was probably right. The times in which Ishii Shiro lived were extreme. Being born during changing times, Ishii was a product of a feudal Japan evolving into industrialization. Western medicine had arrived in Japan not long before his birth.

Ishii Shiro was born on June 25th, 1892 in the village of Chiyoda, Kamo district, Chiba prefecture.

Shiro, meaning "fourth son" in Japanese, was the fourth son of the biggest landowner in the region. His family exercised feudal control not only toward the villagers, but also over the region even after feudalism was supposedly over.

Given his privileged childhood, he was known to be arrogant and brash even in his young days in primary school. However, since he was intelligent and was known to memorize books cover to cover, he was a teacher's favorite despite his behavior.[6]

Given the situation in Japanese education, one excelled in school not only through merit but also through patriotism. By the time Ishii was a teenager, he was fanatical about being loyal to the emperor and to the country as the Imperial Way. Similar to many boys his age, he aspired to become a member of the military. Before he turned 24, he was accepted into the Medical Department of Kyoto Imperial University. Since he was a brilliant student, he quickly attracted the professors' attention. Since Western medicine was new in Japan, there was no need for an ethics class while Ishii was in school. By December 1920, he graduated from the Medical Department of Kyoto Imperial University at age 28. Eager to serve in the military, he began his military training in the Third Regiment of the Imperial

---

[6] Morimura, Seiichi, *The Devil's Gluttony*, Vol. 1, Tokyo: Kadokawa Shoten, 1983, p. 249.

Guard Division. On April 9th, 1921, Ishii began his commission as a Surgeon-First Lieutenant and, on August 1, 1922, he was transferred to the First Army Hospital in Tokyo.

In Tokyo, Ishii had a reputation as a womanizer who frequented geisha houses on a regular basis. Even with his low military pay, he was a generous tipper and was popular among young geishas, often being seen with only young ones about 15 or 16 years old. He was often drunk and complained loudly about the lack of opportunities for a physician to climb the military ladder.[7] His attitude and loud complaints caught the attention of superiors who granted him postgraduate studies back at Kyoto Imperial University where his advanced studies were focused on bacteriology, serology, pathology, and preventive medicine. He was sent to Shikoku Island to study a new disease claiming thousands of lives, developed a water filtration system, and was introduced to the world of epidemic prevention.[8]

Dr. Ishii Shiro was an atypical post-graduate student who acted differently from the other students. One of the professors, Kimura, who was also Ishii Shiro's senior thesis advisor, recalled, "Ishii was something else. He could use test tubes and appa-

---

[7] Ibid., p. 250-254.

[8] Williams, Peter, and Wallace, David, *Unit 731: Japan's Secret Biological Warfare in World War II*, New York: Free Press, 1989, p. 5-6.

ratus that other students had washed clean at night. He came at night because he was lodging in the village of Kawahara. At that time, there were 30 or 40 research students, and they had to be careful to share the laboratory equipment because there wasn't enough to go around. He would come at night to do his work after everyone else left." Not only was he hard working, he liked to promote himself to the higher ups to further his ambition. He not only charmed most of the faculty at the time, but also made himself known to the University President, Araki Torasaburo. Visiting Araki frequently, he was able to network and eventually married Araki's daughter to climb the ladder by acquiring a powerful father-in-law.[9]

By early 1927, he wrote his senior thesis on "Research on Gram Positive Twin Bacteria" and received his doctorate degree in microbiology. At the time of graduation, he held the rank of Captain. After graduation, Ishii Shiro actively participated in the scientific community for biological research. Even with his busy home life, research work, and networking, he still frequented geisha houses and local bars. He eventually stumbled upon the report of the Geneva Protocol and the conference reports

---

[9] Tsuneishi, Kei'ichi and Asano, Tomizo, *The Bacteriological Warfare Unit and the Suicide of Two Physicians*, Tokyo: Shincho-Sha Publishing Co., 1982, p. 132.

of Harada Toyoji and other military doctors and was impressed with the potential for chemical and biological warfare in future war strategy. During World War I, the German army's use of chemical weapons inflicted heavy civilian casualties. Consequently, 44 countries passed an agreement at the 1925 Conference on Disarmament in Geneva on June 17, 1925 and signed an international protocol named "Protocol for the Prohibition of the Use in War of Asphyxiating, Poisonous or other Gases, and of Bacteriological Methods of Warfare" ("Geneva Protocol), prohibiting the use of chemical and biological weapons in war. Representatives from Japan were also present at this conference and were involved in drafting and signing the Geneva Protocol, although it was not ratified in Japan at the time.

At the suggestion of his university mentor, Kiyano Kenji, Ishii Shiro traveled to 25 Western countries in a span of two years starting from April 1928. One of Ishii's colleagues, Kitano Masaji, commented on Ishii's trip with a bit of envy. "The pushy Ishii decided he would take off on his own to Europe.... Ishii paid out of his own pocket for the study abroad at first, and only received official expenses later." The countries included Singapore, Ceylon, Egypt, Greece, Turkey, Italy, France, Switzerland, Germany, Austria, Hungary, Czechoslovakia, Belgium, Holland, Denmark, Sweden, Norway, Finland, Polance, the Soviet

Union, Estonia, Latvia, East Prussia, Hawaii, Canada, and the United States. Some countries were more secretive about their research. However, MIT in the United States was more open about their research. After the visit, Ishii believed that Japan was behind and needed to engage in biological warfare research. Four months upon returning to Japan, Ishii Shiro became an instructor at the Imperial Japanese Army Medical School (IJA Medical School). Japan was a country which lacked mineral resources, making biological weapons a brilliant choice since they were inexpensive and not very costly to produce; at least that was his argument. Moreover, there were transmission factors and the high lethality potential to consider. Therefore, the ultra-nationalistic Ishii Shiro, deciding to lobby the Army Central, proposed establishing a military agency to develop biological weapons for Japan's national interests. One of his most compelling arguments to his superiors was, "that biological warfare must possess distinct possibilities, otherwise, it would not have been outlawed by the League of Nations." At first, his conclusion received no support from the military, but he was able to find a supporter for his cause.

Ishii finally caught the attention of Koizumi Chikahiko, an ultra-nationalist serving as Japan's Minister of Health. With his support in August of 1932, an Epidemic Prevention Laboratory headed by Ishii

Shiro was approved. However, at the time, the Imperial Japanese Army Medical School already had an Epidemic Prevention Laboratory.

In Tokyo, Ishii experienced tremendous success with Koizumi's support. He was able to secure a 1795 square meter complex at the Army Medical College. Since many of his peers were antagonized by him, he was greatly concerned about conducting research at Japan's capital at the time. There was no way he could capture human experimental subjects for vaccine and defensive research work. The type of work which Ishii wanted to do needed to be done outside of Japan proper and the territory of Manchuria looked perfect. In the summer of 1932, after Ishii and his childhood friend, Masuda Tomosada, took a tour to Harbin, Ishii saw Manchuria as a perfect place for his scientific advancement.[10]

---

[10] Harris, Sheldon, *Factories of Death: Japanese Biological Warfare, 1932-1945, and the American Cover-up*, London and New York: Routledge, 1994, p. 15-21.

Chapter 2

Establishment in Manchuria

Dr. Ishii Shiro's plan required considerable funding, something only the Emperor of Japan at the time could approve. Fortunately for Ishii, Emperor Hirohito was a biologist and his love of science became evident in the fourth year of his regency in 1925. Hirohito had a small, well-equipped biological laboratory constructed within the Akasaka Palace, and three years later, in 1928, he had the Imperial Biological Research Institute built within the Fukiage Gardens.[11]

As an ambitious young researcher, Ishii needed a large scale unit where he could roam free. This could have only been done in Manchuria. Despite Japan experiencing an economic depression, he was provided an annual budget of 200,000 yen with a con-

---

[11] Bix, Herbert, *Hirohito and the Making of Modern Japan*, New York: Harper Perennial, 2000, p. 60.

sistent yearly increase even when other units were suffering from budget cuts.[12] It was a sign of how effectively charming Ishii was or how promising his presentations were.

Due to confidentiality surrounding the biological weapons research, Ishii used the alias "Tōgō Taro." Togo Heihachiro was one of Ishii's favorite war heroes and the greatest naval strategist who brought Japan victory over Russia during the Russo-Japanese War. Ishii adapted the name Captain Togo Hajime.

He initially built a garrison facility in Beiyinhe, a village about 70 kilometers southeast of Harbin known as the Zhong Ma Complex. One day in 1932, Ishii and the Japanese army entered the village and evacuated the entire block where Xuan Hua and Wu Miao intersected. They occupied a multi-use structure which had supported 100 Chinese vendors selling clothes and food to the local villagers and set up a temporary site. In 1932, Saburō Endō, Director of Operations of the Kwantung Army, once inspected the "Tōgō Unit." In his book, *The Fifteen Years' Sino-Japanese War and Me*, he described it as follows:

> [It was] converted from a rather large soy sauce workshop, surrounded by high rammed earth wall. All the attending military doctors had pseudonyms, and they were strictly regulated

---

[12] Harris, Sheldon, *Factories of Death*, p. 23.

and were not allowed to communicate with the outsiders. The name of the unit was "Tōgō Unit." One by one, the experimental subjects were imprisoned in a sturdy iron lattice and inoculated with various pathogenic bacteria to observe changes in their condition. They used prisoners on Harbin's death row for these experiments. It was said that it was for national defense purposes, but the experiments were performed with appalling brutality and the dead were burned in high-voltage electric furnaces, leaving no trace.[13]

Inside these walls, Ishii was ruthless. Since he had an unlimited supply of "bandits" or "criminals" to experiment on, he did not keep his prisoners for more than a month. If he needed a brain specimen, his guards would enter a cell where prisoners were kept and smash open a prisoner's brain before discarding the remains in the crematorium.

Due to the Russo-Japanese relationship at the time, Ishii's work was especially important regarding the potential for border disputes along the Manchurian Soviet border. The border was also known for its natural plague area. It was at Beiyinhe, when Ishii experimented on captured bandits using cholera and

---

[13] Japan-China Book Publisher, 1974, p. 162.

plague infected fleas, that he realized their effectiveness as biological weapons.[14]

Because such activities were prohibited by international law, out of consideration for actual combat and taboo in human relations, the Tōgō Unit established a strict security system to keep its research highly confidential. Surprisingly, during the Mid-Autumn Festival on the 15th day of the 8th lunar month in 1934, 16 Chinese prisoners escaped from prison, making it difficult for the Tōgō Unit to sustain its confidential nature. Of the 16 Chinese people who escaped, 12 fled to the Third Route Army of the Northeast Anti-Japanese United Army. After learning about the situation, the Third Route Army from the Chinese Communist Party attacked the Tōgō Unit in Beiyinhe. According to Japanese documents from that time, there were Japanese casualties after the attack. After the prison break incident, the secret was out. The Tōgō Unit closed its operations at Beiyinhe to prevent further disclosure of internal secrets. They first withdrew to the Army Military Medical School in Tokyo but later moved to Nangang, Harbin.

---

[14] Harris, Sheldon, *Factories of Death*, p. 27-28.

基本動作、應用動作ニ關スル學術ヲ教育シ剛健ナル氣力、體力ヲ養成シ白兵ノ使用ニ習熟セシム

　　　第四章　成績報告

第二十五條　本教則第八條ニ據リ教官ニ甲種、乙種及丙種學生ニ就キ試驗ヲ實施シ其成績ハ點數ヲ以テ之ヲ示シ擔任課目數育終了後二週間以内（最終教育課目ニ在リテハ教育終了三週間前）ニ關係教育主任（教官）ヨリ又甲種學生ノ専攻成績ハ各擔任教官ヨリ教育終了三週間前ニ校長ニ提出スルモノトス

校長ハ前項ノ成績ヲ點檢綜合シ列序ヲ附ス

第二十六條　學生ノ教育状況ハ教育終了後直ニ教育主任（教官）ヨリ之ヲ校長ニ提出シ校長ハ教育終了後一ヶ月以内ニ教育實施ノ概況ヲ醫務局長ヲ經テ陸軍大臣ニ報告ス

内科學教室ニ於テハ前年一月軍陣内科ノ大使命トシテ軍隊結核ニ關スル各種ノ研究ヲ課セラレ、之ガ早期發見、豫防ヲ急務トシテ研究實施ニ移リ、教官中村軍醫監主宰ノ下ニ東京第一衞戍病院看護兵ニ就キ調査研究ヲ實施セシガ、之ガ研究ハ一組下ニ於ケル國軍衞生上ノ焦眉ノ急務タルニ鑑ミ、更ニ本年三月改メテ三木軍醫監主宰ノ下ニ内科學教室職員全員ハ東京第一衞戍病院内科病室及兵舍關係職員ノ熱心ナル協力ヲ得テ同病院看護兵ニ就キ精細ナル検査ヲ實施シ、更ニ十月伊吹軍醫正ヲ主任トシテ近衞師團兵ニ就キ同様ノ研究調査ヲ擧セリ。

昭和六年乃至九年事變ニ於ケル滿洲事變ノ功績ニ關シタ各種ニ亙ル功績上申中ニ處、本校高等官職員ニハ之レ昭和七年九月十六日ヨリ同十一年八月三十一日ニ亙ル間ニ於テ行賞令セラレタル者學校長以下七十九名アリ。行賞ノ饗典ハ昭和九年四月二十九日附ニシテ敍勳ト同日附ヲ以 テ夫々昭和六年乃至九年事變從軍記章ヲ授與セラレタリ。

本年中本校職員ニシテ戰死又ハ殉職セシ者左記四名アリ。

　　　左　　記

本籍　千葉縣山武郡千代田村大里加茂一四五一

嘱　託　田　下　五　郎

明治四十二年四月一日生

二一〇

昭和十年七月十八日滿洲國濱江省雙城縣藍梭子溝（背陰河東南方約四粁）ニ於テ匪賊討伐中左胸部穿透性貫通銃創ヲ受ケ戰死。

本籍　千葉縣山武郡千代田村大里一四五一

嘱　託　田　下　丑　之　助

大正二年九月十一日生

昭和十年六月五日滿洲國濱江省雙城縣李家瓦房（背陰河東南方三粁）ニ於テ匪賊討伐中頭部貫通銃創ヲ受ケ戰死。

本籍　千葉縣山武郡千代田村大里一四五一

嘱　員　荻　原　　豊

大正八年三月二十四日生

昭和十年六月二十五日腸チブス」ニ罹リ同日東京第二衛戍病院ニ入院同年七月二十九日東京第二衛戍病院ニ入院同年七月二十九日死亡。

本籍　秋田縣南秋田郡土崎港町清水町六〇

嘱　員　渡　邊　瀨　吉

明治四十一年一月二十八日生

昭和十年六月二十四日腸チブス」ニ罹リ同日東京第二衛戍病院ニ入院同年七月二十六日死亡。

十二月二十七日午後二時ヨリ築地本願寺ニ於テ壯嚴裡ニ葬儀並慰靈祭ヲ執行セリ。

昭和十一年

陸軍軍醫學校五十年史

八月以來從來陸軍省醫務局ノ内陸軍軍醫団ニ於テ編纂發行シアリタル軍醫団雑誌ノ編纂業務ヲ陸軍軍醫學校ニ移管セラレタルヲ以テ、學校幹事三木軍醫監ヲ編纂委員長トシ、副委員長、委員ヲ任命シ陣容ヲ整ヘ益々其堅實ナル發展ノ爲邁進スルコトトナレリ。

本年六月十一日靜岡縣濱松市ニ於テ二千六百名ノ患者發生シテ死亡者四十三名ヲ出シ、陸軍側ニ飛行第七聯隊、高射砲聯隊、濱松陸軍飛行學校等合計四十二名ノ患者發生セリ。濱松衛戍病院長安倍軍醫正ノ急報ニ依リ、醫務局長ハ病原ノ究明及研究員ノ現地派遣ヲ軍醫學校長ニ命ジ、軍醫學校長ハ北野教官以下數名ヲ現地ニ急行セシムルト共ニ、病原ヲ認メラル大編鮮及患者ノ糞便、吐瀉物ヲ蒐集シテ防疫教室ニテ檢索セシメタルガ、現地及教室共ニ病原ハダルトネル氏菌ナルコトヲ確認シ、同月十四日之ヲ公表シテ濱松市ヲ始メ全國ノ非常ナル不安ヲ一掃セリ。十一日患者發生以來流言蜚語頻出シテ一般ニ

人心恟々タリ。名古屋醫科大學、内務省衛生技師、傳染病研究所技師、其他各方面ノ細菌學、法醫學ノ權威者續々濱松市ニ集リ、薔薇狀行ニテ病原ノ究明ニ努メタルモ、混沌トシテ其因不明ノ間ニ、我ガ陸軍軍醫學校ノ一ヲ達(ダルトネル氏菌ヲ蔓延中ニ發見シ、茲ニ世人ハ始メテ我ガ陸軍醫學ガ現代日本ノ醫學ノ淵藪シ居ル實狀ヲ認識シテ驚嘆シ愕クニ至レリ。

陸軍軍醫學校校舎ハ昭和四年現在地ニ移轉セシガ、爾來學生ノ增加ニ伴ヒ漸次狹隘ヲ告グルニ到リシヲ以テ、小泉醫務局長ハ東京第一衛戍病院及軍醫學校自動車庫ヲ他ニ移轉シテ此地ニ建築費豫算二十五萬圓ヲ以テ八十ノ病舍ヲ有スル新病棟ヲ新築スルコトニ決定シ、本年九月上旬工ヲ起シ、十月一日寺師學校長以下關係學校職員、大藏省關係職員竝西村組工事關係者參列ノ下ニ壯嚴ナル地鎮祭ヲ行ヒ、昭和十一年三月下旬竣工ヲ以テ目下着々工事進捗中ナリ。因ニ新病棟ノ地

昭和十年十二月五日陸軍學校附一等軍醫石井榮ハ滿洲ニ於テ關東軍特種任務ヲ帶ビ調製討伐ニ參加シ、常闌(拉濱線山河屯東南方約二千粁)附近ノ關東軍實施病院ニ入院シ、後東京第一衛戍病院ニ遭送セラレ加療中ノ處、本年二月一日卒去ス。依ニ二月七日午後三時ヨリ築地本願寺ニ於テ學校葬ヲ營ミ其位靈對ムル所アリタリ。

二二六

Although the secret was out, Ishii's inventions gained him recognition in the science community. The 1930s was a great decade for Ishii. As was his personality, he boasted about his supposed progress and medical advancement in Beiyinhe. He was so proud of his invention, he peed into the water filter and offered Emperor Hirohito a drink from his filtered urine during a visit in 1933. The Emperor refused his offer and he allegedly drank his own filtered urine.[15] He was flying between Manchuria and Japan giving lectures at both Kyoto Imperial University and Tokyo Army Medical College as well as lobbying military High Command and recruiting students from colleges. Of course, Dr. Ishii Shiro maintained a work-life balance by never letting work get in the way of his pleasure. At this point in his life, he was raising a large family, overseeing research at Beiyinhe, lobbying military commanders, recruiting the brightest minds in Japan, and frequenting the geisha houses. On August 1, 1935, he was promoted to Surgeon-Lieutenant Colonel.

The world did not have much research on biological weapons so it was hard for Ishii's enemies and his peers to question his presentations. His amazing showmanship served to be very convincing regarding his research during his presentations. On May

---

[15] Behr, Edward, *Hirohito: Behind The Myth*, New York: Villard Books, 1989, p. 164.

30, 1936, the Tōgō Unit, also known as the "Kamo Unit", led by Shirō Ishii was awarded the "Army Regulation 'A' No. 7" i.e., confidential military matters of the Japanese army by the Emperor and became an official army. With such a large unit and budget, it seemed that Ishii must have had friends in the highest of places in Japan. It was no longer an agency part of the Epidemic Prevention Institute of the Army Military Medical School but was directly under the Kwantung Army. Moreover, it established a large base in Pingfang district: Central Epidemic Prevention and Water Purification Department of the Kwantung Army for the formal formation and adaptation of the army under the order of the Japanese Central Army. On August 1, 1936, Ishii was appointed as Chief of the Kwantung Army Boeki Kyusui Bu, which meant, Anti-Epidemic Water Supply and Purification Bureau.[16]

His invention not only earned him a boost in the military, he was able to sell it to private companies and sold his water filter design to the Nippon Tokushu Kogyo Kabushiki Kaisha company. The company's water filter manufacturing plant was conveniently located near Ishii's Tokyo laboratory. For the design, Ishii earned a handsome consulting fee of 50,000 yen, notably merely a slight hint of his corrupt career.[17]

---

[16] Harris, Sheldon, *Factories of Death*, p. 31.
[17] Williams, Peter, and Wallace, David, *Unit 731*, p. 11.

In 1939, the Battles of Khalkhin Gol broke out as a consequence of Soviet-Japanese border conflicts. This conflict was named after the river Khalkhin Gol where the battles mostly took place. As the Kwantung Army was located in Manchuria, they were deployed for the battle. As an opportunist, Ishii used this incident to test his biological warfare theories. The Ishii Unit showed off their defensive water filter since he was the expert in water purification at the time. Although Ishii's Unit was present, a large number of Japanese soldiers still died from open wounds and 30% of the deaths were caused by dysentery, which the Japanese believed was caused by an aerial bomb of the Soviets.[18]

Ishii had lobbied the military leaders into allowing him to deploy biological warfare against the Soviets. However, his superiors did not allow such tactics until they were about to lose. Ishii then executed his strategy. In August of 1939, toward the end of the war, his superiors approved. He used 24 of his Youth Corps recruits as "suicide squads" to drop pathogens onto the Soviet side of the Holsten River, a tributary of the Halha River. All of his Youth Corps recruiters were from his same village, so even in the war field, he was able to employ his feudal status on fellows from

---

[18] Coox, Alvin D. *Nomonhan: Japan Against Russia, 1939*, Stanford: Stanford University Press, 1990, p. 1167.

his region[19] Although his efforts were too little too late, he did demonstrate that biological weapons could work against enemies and allowed the empire to explore this particular method for future tactical warfare. The data on this attack was incomplete and it is not clear how many Soviet soldiers actually suffered from the attack, meaning that casualties were not widespread enough for the official data to be tracked. This could have been due to the typhoid bacillus and other pathogens losing their effectiveness in a large body of water such as a river. However, the combat did backfire and at least one Japanese soldier lost his life after becoming infected when he spilled liquid from a drum filled with contaminated water while dumping it into the river. He died of typhoid fever in Hailar at an army hospital.[20]

After the affair, the Ishii Unit received a special commendation from the Kwantung Army Commanding General. On April 29th, 1940, he received a 3rd Order of the Golden Kite and the Middle Cord of the Rising Sun for his service at the Nomonhan Incident.[21]

---

[19] Harris, Sheldon, *Factories of Death*, p. 75.

[20] Tsuneishi, Kei'ichi, "Unit 731 and the Japanese Imperial Army's biological warfare program," In *Japan's Wartime Medical Atrocities: Comparative Inquiries in Science, History, and Ethics*, New York: Routledge, p. 21-31, https://apjjf.org/-Tsuneishi-Keiichi/2194/article.html.

[21] Harris, Sheldon, *Factories of Death*, p. 98.

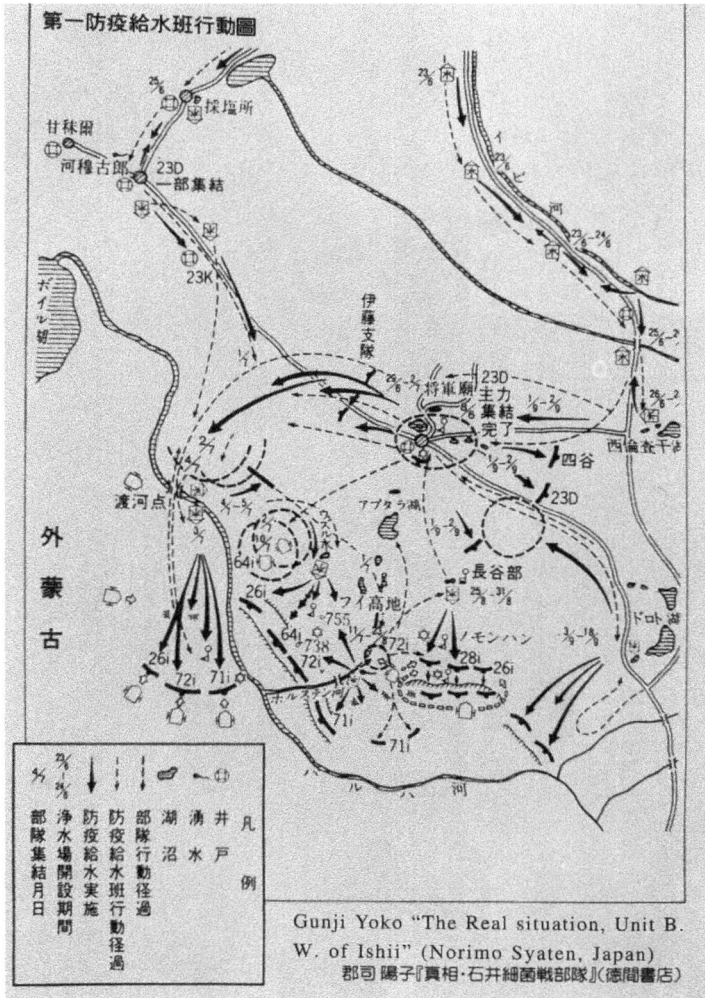

Gunji Yoko "The Real situation, Unit B. W. of Ishii" (Norimo Syaten, Japan)

郡司 陽子『真相・石井細菌戦部隊』(徳間書店)

Chapter 3

Pingfang, Harbin

Throughout the expansion of the Japanese Empire, Ishii's reach expanded with it. He was able to build his network with its headquarters named Ping Fan located 24 kilometers south of Harbin. Ping Fan was in reality a cluster of 10 combined villages. The Imperial Japanese Army used force to sweep the villagers out from 144 acres in 1936, underpaying for their land and forcing them into poverty during cold Manchurian winters.

Abusing his power, Ishii granted Nihon Tokushu-Kogyo Co. Ltd. a monopoly to supply the unit with all necessary equipment and, in turn, he received a handsome kickback. Suzuki, a Japanese construction company, worked day and night when possible, but due to Manchuria's weather, there were times when it was impossible to do so since everything had iced over. Chinese laborers who were hired to construct the complex were denied any basic human rights and wore rags even during cold weather. Some died from the cold and were tossed into a pit, their clothes and valuables passed on to the next laborers who needed them. The laborers slept in tents that barely sheltered them from the winter and meals consisted of pickled vegetables and dumplings. There was almost no difference in the attitude toward the Chinese laborers and the subjects of experiments. Since there were so many Chinese, it did not matter if one or two died because there would always be others.

All equipment for Ping Fan came from the United States or Europe. Having a project of such grand scale, Ishii was in control of an annual budget of at least ten million yen though merely a Lt. Colonel in the Medical Corps in 1936.[22] His life in Manchuria was lavish as he commuted to work in a limousine. His residence in Harbin was a sequestered Russian mansion for his wife and their seven children.[23]

Here is a picture of Ishii's young family in Manchuria in 1938.

---

[22] Ibid., p. 38-39.
[23] Ibid., p. 53.

Ishii had always been known as ambitious and Ping Fan was no small scale laboratory. It consisted of 76 buildings in the base compound with a library, bar, state of the art dormitory buildings, warehouses, brothel, and Shinto shrine; it resembled a city within itself with special tunnels for railroads. Civilian airlines were not allowed to fly into the territory and violators were to be shot down. Locals were told Ping Fan was only a lumber mill and most were too afraid to ask questions. The role of prison warden was assigned to Ishii's own brother, Mitsuo, to ensure no secret leaked out.[24]

---

[24] Tsuneishi, Kei'ichi, *The Germ Warfare Unit that Disappeared: The Kwangtung Army's 731st Unit*, Arlington, VA: US Army Intelligence and Threat Analysis Center, 1982, p. 48.

During the opening of Ping Fan, Ishii addressed his employees in the following speech, "Our god-given mission as doctors is to challenge all varieties of disease causing microorganisms; to block all roads of intrusion into the human body; to annihilate all foreign matter resident in our bodies; and to devise the most expeditious treatment possible. However, the research work upon which we are now about to embark is the completely opposite of these principles, and may cause us some anguish as doctors. Nevertheless, I beseech you to pursue this research, based on the dual thrill of 1), a scientist to exert efforts to probing for the truth in natural science and research into, and discovery of, the unknown world and 2), as a military person, to successfully build a powerful military weapon against the enemy."[25] His speech often soothed the scientists with the greatest doubts as to why they were spending their efforts on harmful weapons instead of curing people.

As the war front expanded throughout Asia after 1937, subsidiary units associated with Ishii's Unit started to appear in Asian cities and towns. These units were under the cover of Epidemic Prevention and Water Supply Departments. In 1938, Unit 1855, otherwise known as the Central Epidemic Preven-

---

[25] Han, Xiao, and Zhou, Deli, "Record of Actual Events of the Bacteriological Factory in Ping Fan," *People's China*, Vol. 3 (1971), passim.

tion and Water Purification Department of the North China Army was established in Beijing. By 1938, Ishii Shiro was promoted to the rank of Colonel. In 1939, Unit 1644 was established in Nanjing and Unit 8604 in Guangzhou. Notably, by the end of 1939, right before the establishment of the Singapore unit, Ishii's network comprised a total of 10,045, of which 4,898 were assigned to the core units in Tokyo and Ping Fan. On March 26, 1942, Singapore's Unit 9420 was established. There were other detachments for biological weapons including Detachment 673 in Sunwu, Detachment 543 in Hailar, and Detachment 162 in Linkou.

At the time, the Japanese army internally referred to the units related to Ishii's biological warfare and the epidemic prevention laboratory of the IJA Medical School as the "Ishii Network" and considered the epidemic prevention laboratory as its research center. This laboratory connected researchers from both inside and outside the military and organized and mobilized the Japanese medical community and civilian research organizations to participate in military medicine and epidemic prevention, including research related to biological warfare, in the form of commissioned research, joint research, paper guidance, and more. Many of the doctoral dissertations done in Japan's medical field at the time sprang

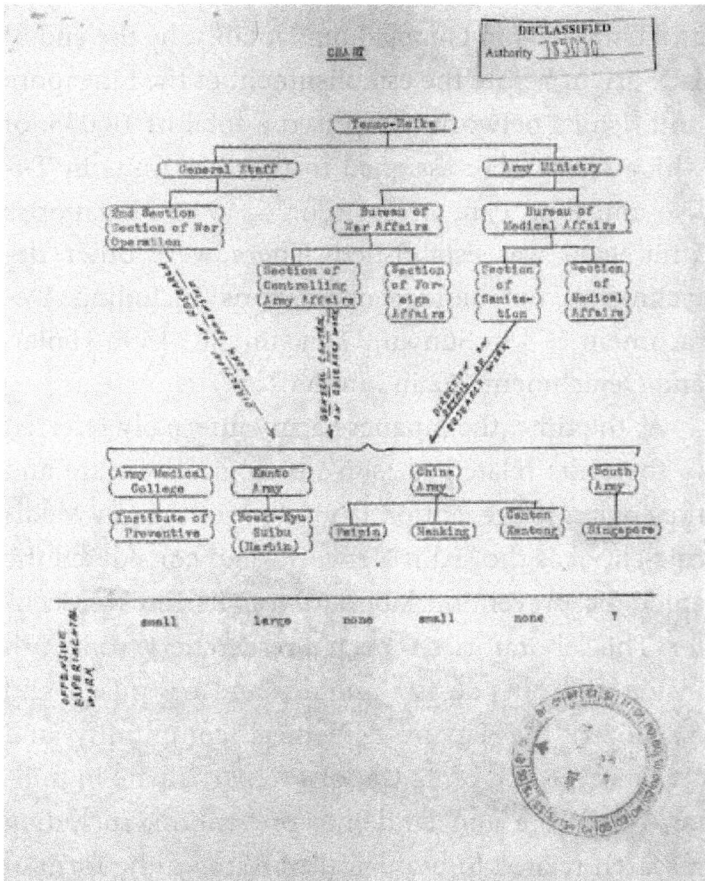

from field tests from Ishii's Network. Japanese researchers spent time as visiting scholars at Unit 731 conducting human experimentation and more for advances in the medical fields of the Empire. Human experimentation at the time was an open secret in Japan. Most of the papers were labeled with Manchurian monkeys as test subjects but nearly everyone in the scientific community knew the reports were based on real human experimentation.[26]

Human experimentation included vivisection, pressure chamber testing to determine survival in planes, and vaccines and defensive work. The victims were treated like logs, or "maruta", in order to dehumanize them. Since they were labeled as maruta, there was a total lack of individuality and they were not seen as humans. They were referred to simply as Maruta Number X and were cremated immediately after their bodies were exhausted from experimentation. When the number became too large, the count was restarted. Therefore, it is hard to know the exact number of victims who died from Ishii's network of human experimentation.[27]

Ishii fostered a culture of total disregard for human life and the consequences of human experimentation. One of his subordinates, Ryouchi Naito,

---

[26] Tsuneishi, Kei'ichi, *Unit 731: The Truth about Biological Weapons and Crimes,* Tokyo: Kodansha, 1995.

[27] Gold, Hal, *Unit 731 Testimony,* p. 41-44.

was using all methods possible to try to obtain a Yellow Fever strain from the Rockefeller Institute. His profile was typical of an Ishii associate. A graduate of Kyoto Imperial University in 1931, he became a medical officer the same year. He entered his alma mater's graduate school for postgraduate studies in 1934 and later became a member of the epidemic prevention laboratory and Second Commander of the Japanese Army Unit 1644 in Nanjing, a biological weapons factory. Dr. Naito edited and published research notes of the members of the biological warfare unit and commissioned scholars for Reports on Epidemic Prevention. He was engaged in researching vacuum drying technology and held an important position in the Ishii Network. Here is the document from the Rockefeller Institute on how Naito attempted to obtain the strain.[28]

---

[28] National Archives, RG 112, E295A, Box 11.

CONFIDENTIAL

THE ROCKEFELLER FOUNDATION

International Health Division
Wilbur A. Sawyer, M.D., Director

Laboratories of the International
Health Division at the Rockefeller
Institute for Medical Research
York Avenue and 66th Street, N. Y.

January 27, 1941

Confidential

Dear Colonel Simmons:

I received your confidential letter of January 24 and
think that Colonel Fox must have misunderstood me. During the past
years we have received only two requests for virulent yellow fever
virus. One of them came from Dr. M. V. Hargett of the U. S. Public
Health Service in Hamilton, Montana. This request was complied with.
The other was from Dr. G. J. Stefanopoulo, Pasteur Institute, Paris,
which was refused.

What I mentioned in my conversation with Colonel Fox were
the following requests and an incident which occurred two years ago.
For your information I am having a statement, which I prepared at the
time for Mr. Fosdick, copied in this letter as follows:

"On February 23 Dr. Ryoichi Naito, who said that he was an
Assistant Professor at the Army Medical College, Tokio, visited the
laboratory, bring a letter of introduction from the Military Attache
of the Japanese Embassy in Washington. The letter stated that a cable
had been received from the Superintendent of the Institute of Infectious
Diseases of the Tokio Imperial University asking Dr. Naito to secure
strains of yellow fever virus for that institute. When I inquired of
Dr. Naito which strains he wished to have, the reply was that he would
like to have the strain now used for vaccination and also a virulent,
unmodified Asibi strain. I telephoned to Dr. Sawyer and asked for in-
structions in this matter and suggested that Dr. Sawyer see Dr. Naito
personally, which he agreed to do. I asked Dr. Naito to present the
letter of introduction from the Japanese Embassy to Dr. Sawyer.

"Later Dr. Sawyer telephoned to inform me that he had declined
to furnish the virus, basing his refusal on the resolution passed by the
Far Eastern Bureau of the Health Section of the League of Nations and
also by the Far Eastern Congress of Tropical Medicine in which the
governments of India, Netherlands, Siam, and others agreed to prohibit
indefinitely the introduction of yellow fever virus for any purpose
whatever into the Asiatic countries. After visiting Dr. Sawyer Dr.
Naito returned to the Institute and asked a number of questions deal-
ing mostly with yellow fever vaccine. He particularly wanted to know
where the vaccine used in Brazil is prepared. I told him that it was
prepared in our laboratory in Rio de Janeiro, and that that used in
Columbia and Central America was shipped from this laboratory.

CONFIDENTIAL SECRET

Colonel Simmons   2   January 27, 1941

"I introduced Dr. Naito to Dr. Theiler. The others had already gone to lunch. Dr. Naito said that he had spent the last year and a half at the Robert Koch Institute in Berlin working with Dr. Schulzberger on the leptospiras and that upon his return to Japan now he thought he would probably be sent to actual field service in Manchuria."

* * * *

"Three days later, i.e., on Sunday February 26, 1939, Mr. Glasounoff, a technician in our laboratory, arrived at my apartment about 2:00 p.m. and reported the following: In the morning when Glasounoff arrived at work in his car about 8:30, he was signaled to stop by a person unknown to him on the corner of York Avenue and 68th Street just as he was turning into 68th Street. The man was about 25, inconspicuous in appearance, of medium height, with no trace of foreign accent. The man looked at his license number and asked if his name was Glasounoff, and receiving an affirmative reply, said he knew someone who would like to meet him and who had some matters to discuss with him which would be very much to the latter's interest. Glasounoff asked the person's name and was told that he would learn that later when they met. Glasounoff's curiosity was aroused considerably and he thought that this person referred to might have some interesting news regarding his family, and therefore agreed to an appointment. Some time ago a person unexpectedly called at the Rockefeller Institute and brought news from his sister in France from whom he had not heard in several years. Accordingly Glasounoff and the person who stopped his car agreed on meeting the unknown person after Glasounoff had finished his work. The time was set at one o'clock, and the place selected was on Exterior Street (Madame Curie Avenue) on the East River where the Institute wall facing the river begins, or approximately the block between 67th and 68th.

"After finishing his work, which consisted of feeding the animals and taking the temperature of the infected monkeys, at one o'clock Glasounoff proceeded to the appointed place in his car by way of 70th Street. He stopped opposite the Institute animal house wall which is a blind wall and without windows. He parked his car just behind another car which he says bore a New York license number ending in 4648, but he cannot remember the letter section. As soon as he arri another car drove up and parked behind his car. It was then raining very hard and the car windows were steamed so he could not see clearly through his back window the outline of the other car but thinks it was a 1939 Buick and is sure it was a four-door sedan. As soon as this car stopped, a man got out, looked into Glasounoff's car, opened the

~~CONFIDENTIAL~~

Colonel Simmons   3   January 27, 1941

door, and asked whether it was Mr. Glasounoff. Upon receiving
an affirmative answer, he entered Glasounoff's car and sat
beside him on the front seat. The stranger began the conversation
by talking in a general way about Glasounoff's work and then stated
that he also was engaged in research work, that he and another person,
whose name he did not mention but stated he was a very famous scientist,
were working together, but that they were handicapped for the lack of
proper material and said that he thought Glasounoff was the proper
person to help him in securing this material. When Glasounoff stated
that he was not in a position to furnish any material, the man answered
that the material specifically needed was yellow fever virus, Asibi
strain. He said that he knew definitely that Glasounoff would have no
difficulty in securing it. When Glasounoff suggested that the man or
the person for whom he was anxious to secure this material approach
Dr. Sawyer, the man answered that he preferred not to attempt to secure
it through official channels. The answer was that since they are planning to do work similar to that carried out in our laboratory, there
might be jealousy in letting him have it. When Glasounoff refused to
comply with the request, the man offered to pay him for it; in fact he
offered him a check for $1,000 and asked Glasounoff to sign a paper,
the exact nature of which Glasounoff did not know. Upon further
refusal from Glasounoff, the man increased the sum to a total of
$3000, promising $1000 immediately and an additional $2000 when the
material is delivered to him. When Glasounoff told him that he could
not get the virus because all virus is locked in the icebox, the man
suggested that he bleed an infected monkey, desiccate the virus, and
deliver it to him, which he assured Glasounoff he could do while working on Sundays without difficulty. Following Glasounoff's repeated
refusals, the man stated that he had better think it over thoroughly,
before giving his final answer as it would be good for Glasounoff to
comply with this request. In the course of their conversation Glasounoff made a move to reach into the back of the car. The man grabbed
his arm, told him to stay where he was without moving, and removed
the ignition key to the car, putting it into his pocket and repeating
that it would be for Glasounoff's good to comply with the request.
Upon receiving the final refusal, he slammed the car door, returned to
his own car, which had the motor running, and drove off immediately in
a southern direction past Glasounoff's car. Being somewhat frightened
and excited, Glasounoff did not notice the license number of the car.
After the disappearance of the car he returned to the laboratory, walk-
ing through very heavy rain, and telephoned Dr. Theiler in Hastings,
reporting briefly what had occurred, and asked his advice about the
next move. Dr. Theiler recommended reporting the affair to me.

~~CONFIDENTIAL~~   ~~SECRET~~

~~CONFIDENTIAL~~

Colonel Simmons   January 27, 1941

"After listening to Glasounoff's story, I telephoned Dr. Sawyer and asked his opinion regarding the advisability of reporting it to the police. He pointed out that there was a possibility that if reported to the police, a certain amount of newspaper publicity would follow involving the name of the Rockefeller Institute and suggested that I consult Dr. Gasser and Dr. Rivers first. Upon calling Dr. Gasser I learned that he was out of town and was not expected back before Tuesday. Dr. Rivers agreed that it was better not to report to the police but suggested talking the matter over in detail with Mr. Smith Monday and then decide upon further steps. When I reported the results of my calls to Dr. Gasser and Dr. Rivers, Dr. Sawyer suggested calling Mr. Smith, which I did. He too agreed that in informing the police the newspapers would get hold of the matter, and it was his opinion that inasmuch as Glasounoff did not get the license number, the police would have nothing to go on, and that better plans could be made on Monday.

"After this conversation I advised Glasounoff to return home, get his duplicate key for his car, and come into the laboratory Monday morning.

"Glasounoff described the man who met him at one o'clock as being about 40 with a slight mustache. He wore a brown coat, brown hat, and blue suit with a red stripe. On the whole he got the impression that the man was educated, well dressed, and that he had a trace of foreign accent."

Whether there was any connection between the request from Dr. Naito and the episode reported by Mr. Glasounoff we are unable to say. Nevertheless the episode was investigated in detail by Mr. Fosdick himself, and he reported it to the State Department. Mr. Glasounoff was followed by a private detective for several weeks, but nothing more of a suspicious nature was reported.

Six months later, i.e., in August 1939, Dr. Sawyer received a letter from Dr. Miyagawa, Director of the Government Institute for Infectious Diseases at Tokyo, stating that Professor Kobayashi would attend the Third International Congress for Microbiology in September 1939 and requested that we furnish him with yellow fever virus of the strain used for yellow fever vaccine. This request was likewise refused on the basis of the resolution passed by the Far Eastern Bureau of the Health Section of the League of Nations.

CONFIDENTIAL

Colonel Simmons   5   January 27, 1941

Before the present war started, virulent strains of yellow
fever virus, to our knowledge, were used for experimental studies in
the following institutions:

1. Paris, France - Pasteur Institute by Dr. G. J. Stefanopoulo, whose
    work for a number of years was subsidized by The Rockefeller
    Foundation.

2. Amsterdam, Holland - Institute of Tropical Medicine by Dr. Schuffner
    and his co-workers.

3. Antwerp, Belgium - Department of Tropical Medicine at the University
    of Antwerp by Dr. Louis van den Bergh.

4. London, England - Wellcome Bureau of Scientific Research by Dr.
    G. M. Findlay.

5. Boston - Harvard University Medical School by Dr. A. W. Sellards.

6. Rockefeller Foundation Laboratories in:

                          New York
                          Rio de Janeiro, Brazil
                          Bogota, Columbia
                          Entebbe, Uganda.

We have received no information about what happened to the material
in Amsterdam and Antwerp. In Paris we presume it must have been
destroyed for otherwise Dr. Stefanopoulo would not have asked for
fresh material.

                          Sincerely yours

                          /S/ J. H. Bauer

                          J. H. BAUER

Colonel James S. Simmons
Office of the Surgeon General
War Department
Washington, D. C.

JHB:MJH

SECRET

CONFIDENTIAL

The Anda testing ground was built to test the effectiveness of biological weapons. It was located 146 kilometers north of Harbin, requiring that Ishii have a plane to facilitate his commute. A fleet of aircraft was maintained at Ping Fan for commuting as well as delivering germ warfare. Being an experienced pilot, Ishii often used a lighter aircraft just for him and his aide. However, with human test subjects, he used a larger aircraft.[29] At the Anda testing ground, researchers tested biological weapons to ensure the bombs Ishii developed were effective in real life. Victims were tied to stakes while the researchers dropped bacteriological bombs onto the test subjects. According to Kawashima during an interrogation of the Khabarovsk Trial on December 25, "In the summer of 1941, the Chief of the detachment, Ishii, called a conference of all the chiefs of divisions and informed us that an instruction had been received from the Chief of Staff of the Japanese Army, the substance of which was as follows: Detachment 731 had done good work in preparation for bacteriological warfare and, in particular, in the breeding of plague fleas on a mass scale." Plague fleas were of great operational and strategic interest and it was, therefore, instructed that research work in this field should be intensified. The Chief of the detachment

---

[29] Harris, Sheldon, *Factories of Death*, p. 58.

pointed out that one of the detachment's weakest points was its inadequate facilities for breeding fleas on a mass scale, and that "all attention must be focused on the mass production of fleas."

The 2nd division controlled an aircraft unit with specially equipped planes near the Anta testing grounds as well as a section that engaged in the cultivation and breeding of parasites intended to cause plague epidemics. In testimony by Kawashima during the Khabarovsk trial, he stated, "... With the available equipment and its rate of output, the Production Division.... could manufacture as much as 300 kilograms of plague bacteria monthly, or 800 to 900 kilograms of typhoid germs". This was also verified by another accused in the Khabarovsk trial, "... The monthly output of the germ producing division could be raised.... if all its equipment were fully operated, to about 300 kilograms of plague bacteria."[30]

Ishii could be thought of as a scientist, innovator, researcher, military leader, businessman, and great commander. His characteristic charm helped him to climb the ladder. Even with significant responsibilities on his shoulders, he still sought pleasure in his life and was out frequently at night in Harbin. Similar to his life as a student, he was a night owl and called meetings at 2:00 or 3:00 in the morning. His

---

[30] *Khabarovsk Trial*, Vol. 4, p. 286.

subordinates admired his eccentric personality.[31] According to the historian Morimuri Masaichi, Ishii slept during the day but sneaked out at night to Harbin and Shenyang to visit first class geisha houses such as "Powder Hill." He could not be found even when the Kwantung Army commander summoned him in an emergency. This type of behavior could be a source of trouble later on in the war.

---

[31] Hariss, Sheldon, *Factories of Death*, p. 58.

Chapter 4

Failures and Corruption

In the 1930s, Ishii was climbing the military ladder quickly, receiving upgrades every 3 years. In the 1940s, however, his career seemingly started to decelerate. On November 28th, 1940, Ishii's Unit attacked Jinhua with biological weapons. The Chinese Ministry of Health stated, "At the time that the plague epidemics were continuing in Ningbo and its vicinity, three Japanese airplanes flew over Jinhua and dropped a large number of small granules the size of small shrimp eggs. These strange objects were gathered and examined at a local hospital.... They showed the physical characteristics of the bacteria that causes the plague. In any case, the plague did not break out in Jinhua and, as far as this town was concerned, the Japanese experiment in germ warfare ended in failure." The townspeople were likely to have stayed at home. Another theory was that the Chinese Ministry of Health released propaganda to boost the people's confidence.

In the fall of 1941, Ishii's Unit attempted to drop plague fleas from airplanes onto Changde, a city 1000 kilometers east of Shanghai. This attack also resulted in failure. It was apparent that the biological weapons program was not as promising as Ishii had proclaimed.

After Pearl Harbor in 1941, President Roosevelt wanted revenge. However, it was difficult to realize due to the distance between the United States and Japan. The solution was to establish an airfield in China, and Zhejiang was selected. They also chose Doolittle, a pilot known for flying from coast to coast without refueling and who understood efficiency. The Doolittle Raid bombed Tokyo, Kobe, and Yokohama as well as an ammunition factory.[32] The bombers were not successful in damaging the structure but they launched a Zhejiang-Jiangxi Campaign to remove the Zhejiang airfields where Chinese civilians were fueling planes.

The IJA's China Expeditionary Force sent 180,000 men as well as a bacteriological warfare unit to launch a full-scale campaign in the Zhejiang-Jiangxi region, Operation Sei-go, also known as the Zhejiang-Jiangxi

---

[32] Groom, Winston, et al. "Trained in Secret, These Fearless Pilots Retaliated for Pearl Harbor," *75 Years Ago, Doolittle Raid Was Payback for Pearl Harbor*, NationalGeographic.com, 15 Apr. 2017, www.nationalgeographic.com/news/2017/04/doolittle-raiders-anniversary-world-war-two-history/.

Campaign, from mid-May to early September 1942. They spread cholera, typhoid, plague, dysentery, glander, and anthrax in the region. This bacteriological warfare operation was confirmed by Major General Kawashima Kiyoshi who worked at Unit 731 and who stated during the Khabarovsk Trial, "My unit could produce 300 kilos of plague bacteria, 1000 kilos of cholera bacteria, 800-900 kilos of typhoid, and 500-700 kilos of anthrax in a month. In 1942, General Ishii led 150 soldiers to disseminate plague, cholera, typhoid, and anthrax in the Zhejiang-Jiangxi War." In another meeting in 1942, Ishii Shiro stated, "The bacteria weapons used in Zhejiang-Jiangxi War Zone were very effective, causing several fierce epidemics."[33]

The operation had also led to 1700 casualties in the Imperial Japanese Army. At the end of 1944, a Japanese medic captured by American forces stated the following, "When Japanese troops overran an area in which a [biological weapons] attack had been made during the Chekiang [Zhejiang] campaign in 1942, casualties upward from 10,000 resulted within a very brief period of time. Diseases were particularly cholera, but also dysentery and pest [bubonic plague]. Victims were usually rushed to hospitals.... Statistics which POW saw at Water Supply and Purification

---

[33] Chan, Jenny. *The Khabarovsk War Crimes Trial: Unearthing Biological Warfare in WWII*. San Francisco: Pacific Atrocities Education, 2020.

Department HQ at Nanking showed more than 1,700 dead, chiefly from cholera; POW believes that actual deaths were considerably higher, 'it being a common practice to pare down unpleasant figures.'"[34]

In July 1942, Ishii joined Nanking Unit 1644 to distribute typhoid and paratyphoid germs from metal flasks to wells, swamps, and civilian houses. He then visited a local Chinese POW camp to hand out a holiday favor, special dumplings injected with typhoid or paratyphoid germs, after which the prisoners were released to spread the disease, causing an epidemic in the area. He also handed out candies with anthrax for children and left sweet cakes filled with typhoid and paratyphoid bacteria around fences and trees in Nanking. Since the Chinese were starving at the time, they ate anything in front of them.[35]

After Nanking, Ishii disappeared from the limelight of biological warfare grounds from August 1942 to March 1, 1945 and was then transferred to Taiyuan where he assumed the position of Chief of Medicine, Department of the First Army. The rumor regarding his transfer was due to investigation of charges of corruption as well as failure to deliver

---

[34] Kobayashi Hideo, and Kojima Toshiro, eds., *731 saikinsen butai: Chugoku shin shiryo* (*The bacteriological war unit 731: New Chinese documents*), Fuji Shuppan, 1995.

[35] Hariss, Sheldon, *Factories of Death*, p. 77-78.

biological weapons.[36] Historian Fujii Shitsue's theory of Ishii's departure was that it allowed Ishii to focus completely on the development and applications of biological warfare. According to the 2nd Chief of Command of Unit 731, Major General Masaji Kitano, even though Ishii had physically left the Unit, he never lost control of it.

Similar to most things about Ishii, there is an air of mystery to what exactly happened, here is a timeline of his movements during his disappearance. In August 1942, Ishii was appointed as Chief of the Medical Department of the 1st Army in Taiyuan, Shanxi, but Ishii did not take up an official post there. On November 20th, 1942, Ishii took an unknown identity in "Taiyuan Epidemic Prevention Training Class." In December 1942, he inspected the Luan military hospital, and then went missing again. In March 1943, Ishii carried out some inspections in Shanxi in Luan hospital again. In April, he inspected Chunxian and was back in Taiyuan in July where he spoke. In September, he returned to Luan, and never returned to Shanxi where Major General Koudou took over Ishii's position.

According to Hayashi, a member of the Unit 1855 in Beijing, Ishii was a leader of the germ attack in West Shandong in 1943. During this period of

---

[36] Morimura, Seiichi, *The Devil's Gluttony.*

time, Ishii attended every important policy decision conference on biological warfare in Tokyo from 1942 to 1945. In April 1943, the high command held a meeting to discuss the use of biological warfare in Southeast Asia. The Ishii protocol, suggested during the meeting, was to use 27 air bombers to disperse bacteria in Burma, India, South China, New Guinea, and Australia.[37]

The Japanese army general staff started losing confidence in the efficacy of biological weapons, which pressured Ishii's Unit to come up with a new way of delivering a more reliable method of delivering biological weapons for the Japanese soldiers while creating devastating effects for the enemy. The Ishii Unit came up with a new approach, which was to pack the pathogens in bombs or shells and to be dropped by airplanes and artillery. However, packing the bombs with pathogens was not an easy task as it was hard to keep the pathogens alive for long periods of time. Moreover, there was the need to develop a bomb made of materials that could break upon impact using little or no explosives since explosives require heat which could kill the pathogens.

The Ishii Unit was filled with great innovators who figured out the best way was to have a live host,

---

[37] Imoto, Kumao, *Sakusen Nisshi de Tsuduru Daitoasenso* (*The Great East Asian War, written as an Operations Diary*), Tokyo: Fuyo Shobo Shuppan, 1979.

such as a plague flea, inside a porcelain bomb to carry the pathogen. By the end of 1944, this porcelain flea bomb, also known as the Ishii bacterial bomb, was perfected. Ishii's unit technicians were collecting rats from villagers in order to breed more fleas to produce those bombs.[38]

---

[38] Tsuneishi, Kei'ichi, "Unit 731 and the Japanese Imperial Army's biological warfare program."

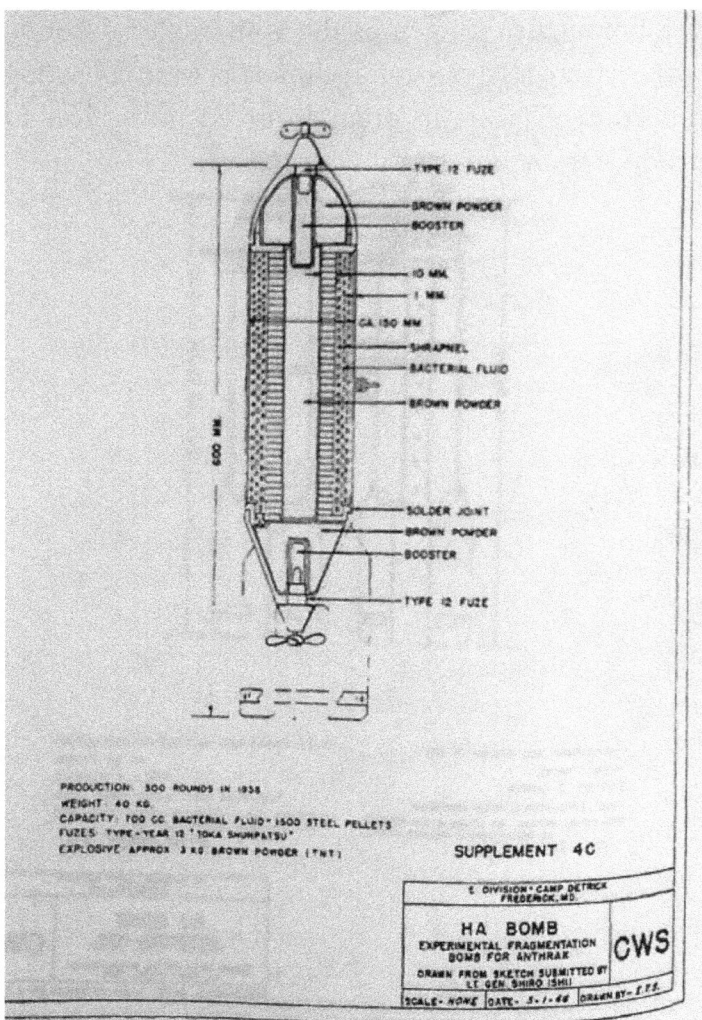

PRODUCTION: 300 ROUNDS IN 1938
WEIGHT: 40 KG.
CAPACITY: 700 CC BACTERIAL FLUID - 1500 STEEL PELLETS
FUZES: TYPE - YEAR 12 "TOKA SHUMPATSU"
EXPLOSIVE: APPROX 3 KG BROWN POWDER (TNT)

SUPPLEMENT 4C

E DIVISION - CAMP DETRICK
FREDERICK, MD.

HA BOMB
EXPERIMENTAL FRAGMENTATION
BOMB FOR ANTHRAX
DRAWN FROM SKETCH SUBMITTED BY
LT. GEN. SHIRO ISHII

CWS

SCALE - NONE   DATE - 3-1-46   DRAWN BY - E.P.S.

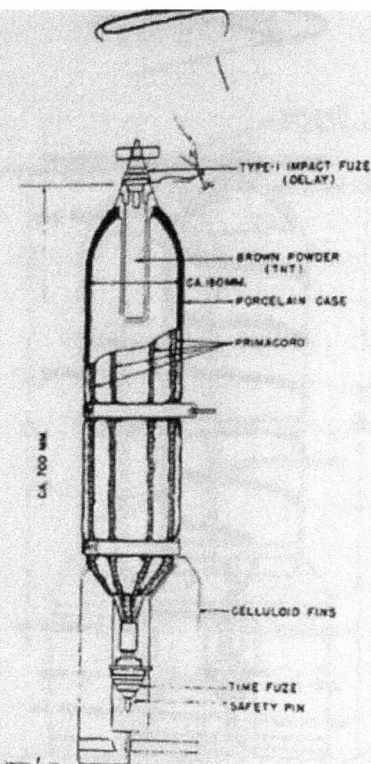

TYPE-I IMPACT FUZE
(DELAY)

BROWN POWDER
(TNT)
CA. 150MM.

PORCELAIN CASE

PRIMACORD

CA. 700 MM

CELLULOID FINS

TIME FUZE
SAFETY PIN

TYPE 50

PRODUCTION- APPROXIMATELY 500 ROUNDS 1940-1941
WEIGHT- 25 KG. CAPACITY- APPROXIMATELY 10 LITERS
FUZE NOSE FUZE- TYPE I IMPACT (DELAY)
    TAIL FUZE- TIME FUZE (REMODELED FROM TYPE
        YEAR 3 COMPLEX FUZE FOR ARTILLERY
        SHELL)
EXPLOSIVE- APPROXIMATELY 4 METERS PRIMACORD AND
    500 GRAMS TNT.

TYPE 100 (SAME DESIGN)

PRODUCTION- 300 ROUNDS 1940-1942
LENGTH- APPROX. 1600 MM. WIDTH-APPROX. 300 MM.
WEIGHT- 50 KG. CAPACITY- APPROX. 25 LITERS
FUZES- (SAME)
EXPLOSIVE-APPROX. 12 METERS PRIMACORD AND
    500 GRAMS TNT

SUPPLEMENT 4 G

C DIVISION-CAMP DETRICK
FREDERICK, MD.

TYPE 50 UJI BOMB
IMPROVED PORCELAIN
EXPERIMENTAL BOMB FOR
BACTERIAL LIQUID
DRAWN FROM SKETCH SUBMITTED BY
LT. GEN. SHIRO ISHII

CWS

SCALE- NONE | DATE- 4-26-46 | DRAWN BY- E.F.S

In the spring of 1945, Ishii was devising a long-distance attack on the United States with the Ishii bacterial bomb. The plan was called "Cherry Blossom at Night", and was to spread plague in San Diego on September 22nd, 1945, but the war ended before the plan could be launched. The operation was a kamikaze mission with Aichi M6A Seiran aircraft carrying plague-infected fleas launched from five I-400 class long-range submarines. The planes were to either drop the plague or to purposely crash in order to disperse the infection to infect the entire West Coast.[39]

---

[39] LoProto, Mark. "The Secret Japanese Plan for Biological Warfare," *Visit Pearl Harbor*, 13 Oct. 2018, https://visitpearlharbor.org/the-secret-japanese-plan-for-biological-warfare/.

Chapter 5

Post-War

The end of the war came as a surprise to everyone at Ishii's Network. Unlike the United States which took its time to occupy Japan, the Soviet Union had rushed into Manchuria. On August 9th, General Yamada, the Commander in Chief of the Kwantung Army, signed an order to destroy Unit 731.[40] The buildings were dynamited and all prisoners were cremated and their ashes cast into the Songhuajiang River outside of Harbin. No prisoners were allowed to survive.[41]

According to one of the nurses, Akama Masako, in the final days of Unit 731, she was, ".... with the syphilitic mothers; the doctor in charge of our team delivered the maruta babies himself instead of having the nurses do it, as would normally be the case. At that time, he would order me to stop the blood flow from

---

[40] *Khabarovsk Trial*, p. 271.

[41] Tsuchiya, Takashi, "Japanese Medical Atrocities 1932-1945: What, Who, How, and Why?" *22nd International Congress of History of Science*, Beijing, July 29, 2005, p. 5.

the mother to the baby. The doctor would take a sample of the blood, then I would let small quantities of blood flow intermittently, as he took successive samples. The test tubes were all lined up on the shelf. He was checking to determine the intensity of the syphilis transmitted from mother to child and the progression of the disease from the time of birth. A researcher came running in, screaming that some maruta had escaped. They were caught by the Special Forces, the team under Ishii Shiro's brother, Ishii Takeo. Only someone who could be trusted was admitted to that team. They shot the escapees.

When it came time to evacuate, we got into a train and left the unit headquarters. It was a long train, maybe twenty or thirty cars. A soldier came running to me and said that a baby was going to be born in a freight car at the end of the train. We ran back through the cars. The wife of one of the unit members was there in labor, and there were soldiers with lots of medals. Surrounded by those high-ranking officers, I delivered the baby. That was August 15, 1945. We were passing through Xinjing. The train engineer ran away and we could not move. Planes were flying overhead, keeping lookout; soldiers were around us. I was trembling in fear. This, I felt, was really war. Then, we heard the emperor's words ending the war. We were always told to "work hard and Japan will definitely win." When I heard that we had lost, I was sad. It grew dark. Ishii came over to us carrying a big candle and said, 'I'm sending you all back home. When you get there, if any one of you gives away the secret of Unit 731, I personally will find you, even if I have to part the roots of the grass to do it.' He had a fearful diabolical look on his face—my legs were shaking—and not just at me—at everyone. 'Even if I have to part the grasses....'"[42]

During the occupation of Japan, General MacArthur became the Supreme Commander for the Allied Powers, SCAP. According to his order, the functions of the Legal Section of the GHQ were to advise him on legal issues and policies related to war crimes and to pursue war criminals. Ishii was one of the most wanted by the United States. Since the United States took its time to occupy Japan, Ishii had time to fake his death and hide some of his documents in his backyard. A newspaper had reported that Ishii was shot to death and the villagers even staged a funeral for him. However, the CIA found him at Kamo Village.[43]

The Japanese Communist Party had sent letters informing the GHQ of Ishii's activities in Manchuria. On December 14th, 1945, the GHQ had filed the following letter:[44]

---

[42] Gold, Hal, *Unit 731 Testimony*, p. 128.

[43] Report of November 10th, 1945 on Ishii's staged funeral in Chiba, National Archives and Records Administration, RG 290, Box 12.

[44] National Archives of the United States, RG 331, B1434.

OCCIO Ops
APO 500
14 Dec 45

MEMORANDUM FOR THE OFFICER IN CHARGE:

Subject: Memorandum from Japanese Communist Party.

The following memorandum was received by the Research & Analysis
Section from the Japanese Communist Party. It is copied below without
change in language. The report is in two sections, the second part relating to General (Rtd.) ISHIHARA Kanji. A quick check of the names
mentioned in the first part of the report, relating to Japanese bacteriological warfare, revealed no record in CIS.

"ACTIVITY OF ISHII B.W.A. CORPS

"Ishii B.W.A. (Bacterial War Army) was established in Harbin under
commandership of Lieutenant-General Shiro Ishii. A large bacterial
laboratory built in Harbin, succeeded in cultivating pest in 1944, December. Pest was applied to Manchurians, in Moukden was applied to several
American citizens captured during war. For experiment sake, rats im-
planted with pest were dispersed in and around Moukden, as a result of
which it was proved successfull. When Ishii after these experiments was
about to start actual manufacturing in large scale war termination was
declared. Japanese army bombarded the laboratory wherein most precious
documents, equipments were destroyed together with hundreds of laboratory
members engaged in study. The research works were conducted in cooperation with Tokyo and Kioto Imperial Universities medical laboratories.

"Most leading personel engaged in this research were Rinnosuke Shoji
and Hisato Yoshimura in the Laboratory and Kiyu Ogata of Chiba Medical
University assisted from outside. In 1944 spring Ryoichi Naito succeeded
to Ishii. Most of medical institutes, universities were mobilised for the
purpose, which are:

```
"Densenbyo Kenkyusho:  Saburo Kojima
                       Shogo Hosoya
                       Hidetake Yahagi
"Kioto Imperial University:  Kozo Kunimoto
                             Shiro Kasahara
"Medical Bureau of War Ministry:  Lieut.-General Hiroshi Kanbayashi
                                  Lieut.-Colonel Hiraga
                                            Asaoka
                                            Kaji
                       Maj.-Colonel Otaguro
                                    Akuzuki
```

An issue of Pacific Stars and Stripes from February 27, 1946 stated the following, "Lt. Gen. Shiro Ishii, head of the Japanese Medical Research Institute, which conducted experiments in certain phases of biological warfare as well as preventive medicine at Ping Fan near Harbin, Manchuria has been located and brought to Tokyo for interrogation after an intensive search by Army intelligence agencies, it was revealed by G-2 SCAP. The search for Gen. Ishii, who has been an important intelligence target, was redoubled early last month following a UP dispatch in the Communist sources with having conducted bubonic plague experiments on American and Chinese POW's.

Shortly thereafter Gen. Ishii was located by the CIC in China Prefecture. An order for him to appear for interrogation was presented to the Japanese and on Jan. 18 he was delivered to SCAP by the Japanese authorities. He was presently living in Tokyo and is not under arrest. Meanwhile, Lt. Col. A. T. Thompson of the Chemical Warfare Service, flew from Washington to Tokyo on a special order to interrogate Ishii."

The report continued, "He was described as a determined, almost ruthless individual who rose from the rank of colonel in 1941 to Lt. Gen. in 1945."[45]

---

[45] Kalisher, Peter, "SCAP Locates and questions General Ishii," *Pacific Stars and Stripes*, Feb. 27th, 1946.

However, Thompson was not a skilled interrogation officer. He had too much admiration for high ranking officers such as Ishii. This is learned from a stenographic transcript of interrogation by Lt. Colonel A. T. Thompson on February 5, 1946 of Dr. Ishii Shiro. One can see that Thompson allowed Ishii to dodge many questions. However, Thompson was able to extract information on the Ishii bacterial bomb. One can come to the conclusion that Ishii was a master politician from the manner in which he answered during interrogation.

Stenographic Transcript of Interrogation
Of Lt. General SHIRO ISHII in Tokyo
By Lt. Colonel A.T. Thompson
On 5 February 1946

A demonstration of the four water purification apparatus and the one culture apparatus was made. General ISHII also present the completed answers to the questionnaire on field trials. He also presented information in chart form on institutions and personnel concerned with BW research. Also presented was a chart giving the titles of experiments or work conducted at the Heibo institute.

Q   You did no BW work except at the Army Medical College and at Heibo?

A.   BW work was done only at HEIBO. Only general preventive medical science was conducted at the Army Medical College.

Q   Was any work done at the Kyoto Imperial University?

A   The professor there did not like that kind of work, so none was undertaken.

Q   The research work was limited to Heibo institute?

A   Only at Heibo. A lot of men in my unit and others who do not know anything about it have been spreading rumors to the effect that some secret work has been carried on in BW and they have gone as far as saying an attack with BW was planned by my unit and that a lot of bacteria were being produced, large quantities of bombs manufactured and airplanes being gathered for that purpose. I want you to have a
clear   understanding that this is false.

Q   In other words, no work was conducted on BW except at the Heibo institute?

A.   That is correct.

Q   Did you expect the enemy to use BW?

A.   In my opinion, some countries might.

Q   Which countries did you expect to use it?

A.   Soviet Union and China. They had used it previously and I expected them   to use it again.

Q.   What did you expect from the United States in the field of BW?

A.   I did not think the United States would use BW.

Q.   Why?

A.   I believed since the United States had money and materials, they would use more scientific methods of warfare.

Q.   Do you think BW is practical?

A.   You have to have much money and materials to create conditions favorable to BW.

Q.   Do you think BW is something that nations will have to contend with in the future?

A.   In a winning war, there is no necessity for using BW and in a losing war, there is not the opportunity to use BW effectively. You need a lot of men,, money and materials to conduct research into BW. There is little data on the effectiveness of BW as a weapon. I do not know whether BW can be used effectively on a large scale. It might be effective on a small scale.

Q.   Do you mean sabotage?

A.   It might be effective in such methods of sabotage as dropping bacteria into wells.

Q.   It might be effective under those conditions?

A.   I believe such methods could be controlled by my methods of water purification. I heard over the radio that Russia had completed its preparations for BW and it frightened me, but I did not know whether it was actual fact or just was printed in "Red Star" or some other newspaper as a "scare." I do not know how far they have advanced in BW and have wondered what they would use if they attacked with BW.

Q.   What bacteria do you think the Russians might use?

A. Tularemia, typhus fever, cholera, anthrax, pest.

Q. What makes you believe that the Russians would use these organisms?

A. I heard reports from people returned from Russia that the Russians had been using these organisms in their preparation for BW.

Q. Would it not be difficult to produce typhus organisms on a large scale?

A. If you could produce a lot of lice you might be able to produce a lot of typhus. German and Polish vaccine is prepared from lice. Trouble with lice is that you have to have human infectious blood to infect the lice. Weil's disease is produced in the same manner and it is very hard to get large quantities. If a country was rich enough, it might be able to make that disease a dangerous weapon.

Q. Was any research conducted on BW against food plants?

A. We did not do any experiments on it. Our work was to protect the soldiers.

Q. Did anyone else concern themselves with BW against crop plants?

A. I do not know.

Q. Were you concerned with BW agents against animals?

A. We did not do any experiments on large animals. We used small animals as test animals. Besides, we had no veterinarians.

Q. Did veterinary laboratories do any research on BW?

A. I do not know. It was such a secret that there was no communication between units. Even personnel working on experiments in my unit did not know what they were working on. Only myself, Colonel MASUDA, and one or two other persons know.

Q. Who were the other persons?

A. There were some who suspected what was going on, but did not know. Colonel MASUDA, Tomosada, and myself know.

Q. What section of the BW institute did the BW work?

A. When those experiments came up, a number of men from each group were picked out to do the work. They were only together temporarily and were disbanded when the experiment was completed.

Q. Were all the people in such groups informed of the nature of the work?

A. They were not informed of what they were doing. They protested that they could not carry on with their own experiments and that their regular work was being interfered with.

Q. Would not more progress have been made if those working on the experiment had been told what it was all about?

A. If they had known what they were working on they would have shrunk up from fright and asked for more pay. They were not well-trained men and were usually picked from the ranks.

Q. A soldier is a soldier and could you not have ordered them to do the work?

A. They were not soldiers. They were reservists. Those in the branch units were soldiers, but not those in the main unit. I could not order them.

Q. How much research cooperation was given by the Navy on BW?

A. There was no cooperation whatsoever.

Q. Did not some naval medical officers attend your lectures at the Army Medical College?

A. No. Naval officers are too proud. They do not have any brains, but their noses are high.

Q. From captured documents, we are given to understand that certain naval personnel received additional pay for hazardous work which included work with bacteria and certain poison gasses. Evidently, the Navy must have had some part in it. Why did one personnel receive extra pay?

A. I received no reports from the Navy and I heard nothing about it. The number of medical men in the Navy is less than 10 per cent of those in the Army and I doubt if they had any men capable of conduction experiments.

Q.   What training is BW was given to the Kempei Tai?

A.   There is a Military Police unit in Nakano-ku which was given training by some medical officers from the Army Medical College. It was just a basic information course on how to discover and report BW incidents.

Q.   Who conducted those courses?

A.   Colonel MASUDA, Tomosada, and Colonel NAITO, Ryoichi.

Q.   Would it be possible to obtain copies of their lectures?

A.   I will try to find out.

Interpreter   : 2nd Lt. F. H. Ellis
Interpreter   : T/Sgt. Toshio Kitamura
Stenographer   : T/4 K. A. Haack

Many who lived in occupied Japan sent letters regarding Ishii's activities in Manchuria. In a letter On November 8th, 1946, an anonymous informant claimed that he had worked under Ishii's supervision during the war. The informant claimed that Ishii was an enemy against humanity and was willing to work with GHQ.[46]

---

[46] National Archives of the United States, RG 331, B1434.

Date: 8 November 1946

Report of Investigation Division, Legal Section, GHQ, SCAP.

Inv. Div. No. 330	CRD No.	Report by: L. H. Barnard, Maj. Inf, O-191697

Title: Motoji YAMAGUCHI with aliases, et al

Synopsis of facts:

Anonymous letter alleges Lt. General Shiro ISHII engaged in activities while in China which would characterize him as a war criminal and involve one member of the Imperial family.

– P –

Reference: Report of Major L. H. Barnard, dated 5 November 1946.

DETAILS:

At Tokyo:

An anonymous letter, dated 3 September 1946, giving an address of Koriyama-shi, Fukushima-ken, was sent to the CIAE Section of SCAP, where a translation was obtained and the original and translation forwarded to the Legal Section for appropriate action.

The original and copies of the translation of same are being transmitted to the Criminal Registry Division with their copy of this report.

The letter reads as follows:

"CIAE, GHQ

Contribution concerning Surgeon Lt.Gen. Shiro Ishii.

I was forced to work in the army for a long time only for victory recently was demobilized without belongings.

People treat me cold-heartedly and I have no job at present, when inflation is rampant. Moreover, I have many family members to feed. This is the whole reward for me, who worked whole-heartedly at the risk of my life.

Distribution:
1 Prosecution ✓
1 CRD (Encl)
1 Fukuoka
1 Osaka
1 Sapporo
1 Chinese Division
3 Inv. Div. (File #330)

Do not write in this space.

B

One year after the termination of war, my living has become more and more difficult. Gradually I have began to lose hope of living through it.

Japan is now endeavouring to become a peaceful country. To realise this aim, militarists must be eradicated completely. But the cabinets since the end of the war have strove to conceal them as best as they could. Now I want to tell you the case of Lt. Gen. Ishii as an example.

A repatriate from Manchuria reported in the newspaper that he was shot to death, but this is not a fact, this article was made by the order of the government and nothing else. He was a well-known militarist and enemy of humanity. He established the Epidemic Prevention and Water Supply Section of Kwantong army. What did he do through this section and what did he plan? I was once attached to his corps, so I know quite well about his work. Militarists are afraid of his summon, as the secrets will be revealed by it. His summoning will provide evidence and data against 'A' class war criminal suspects and even one Imperial family member will be affected. So the cabinets, especially the Foreign Ministry, ex-Army Ministry. Demobilization Board and Liaison Office have endeavored to make this case lost in oblivion. I believe that it is utterly necessary to judge him and those who planned and worked with him fairly for the establishment of truly peaceful country.

I know quite well about him and his corps and the atrocities committed by them.

If you want my help, I will work as best as I can for the investigation of this case.

I have strict confidence to correspond to your expectation, if you permit me certain number of days and expenditures for investigation.

As to details, I want to meet you to consult with you. If you want to make me do this work, please put the following advertisement in the Nippon Keizai Press within 3 days after the arrival of this letter to you.

[Attendance Order !

'Shiro Ishii is required to appear in person on ——day Sept, 1946.

CIAE, GHQ, SCAP.'

The request contained in the letter that the writer be contacted through the Keizai Press, could not have been complied with even had it been desirable, inasmuch as the original letter had not been translated within the specified time.

This information is being included in this report as another indication of the mounting complaints concerning the alleged activities of General ISHII and his associates at the Kwantung Experimental Stables in China, principals among which are alleged to have been infecting Prisoners of War with glanders for experimental purposes.

– 2 –

UNDEVELOPED LEADS:

The Osaka Office — At Kyoto — Will locate and interview Hiroshi UEKI, presently reported residing in Kyoto-shi, Yoshita-cho, and obtain a complete and exhaustive statement from him concerning his knowledge of the matter of the experiments which were allegedly conducted upon Prisoners of War at the HARBIN experimental station.

At Hagi-shi, Yamaguchi-ken, — will locate and interview Shiro YAMASHITA, presently reported residing at 173 Tsuchirara, Hagi-shi, Yamaguchi-ken, concerning his knowledge of the experiments conducted on Prisoners of War.

For the information of the Osaka Office, the service record of NAKAMATSU as set forth in reference report, discloses that he graduated from the Agricultural Department of the Tokyo Imperial University in 1922, subsequently served at the Epidemic Research Institute, had a tour of duty in Germany, served with the Military Service Bureau of the War Ministry, was a former instructor in the Army Veterinary School, was former Chief of the Veterinary Branch of the 13th Army and on 1 July 1942 became Chief of the Quarantine Stables of the Kwantung Army.

The Tokyo Office — At Tokyo — Will report the result of the demand placed on the Japanese Government for the military and biographical history of ISHIMURA and set forth appropriate leads for the location and interview of this individual.

Will report the result of the demand placed on the Japanese Government for the military and biographical history of YAMAGUCHI, YAMASHITA, and ISHII.

At Kofu — Will locate and interview Yatsutaro HOSAKA, presently reported residing at 41 Yoka-machi, Kofu-shi, Yamanashi-ken, concerning his knowledge of the illegal experiments reportedly conducted by the staff of the Quarantine Stables of the Kwantung Army. For the information of the agent conducting this interview, the service record of HOSAKA as reflected in reference report discloses that he was commissioned a Major in the Veterinary Corps on 1 August 1941 and on 31 March 1942 was appointed to the staff of the Research Division of the Army Veterinary School. On 20 August 1942, he was appointed to the staff of the Veterinary Branch of the Kwantung Defense Army and on 22 June 1944 he was appointed to the staff of the Quarantine Stables of the Kwantung Army, He became a Lt. Colonel in the Veterinary Corps on 1 March 1945.

At Tokyo — Will confer with the Chinese Division for the purpose of ascertaining whether they have any information concerning the alleged atrocities committed on Prisoners of War or Chinese Coolies, as indicated in the body of this report.

P E N D I N G

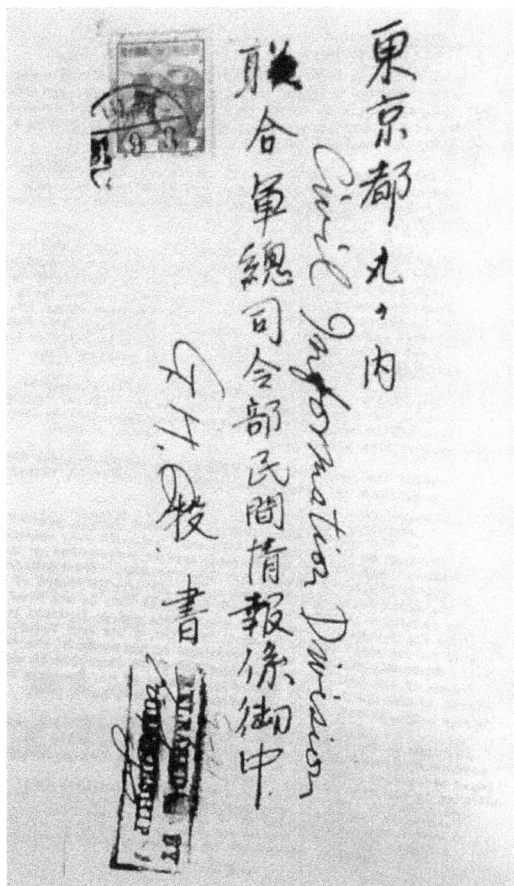

東京都 丸ノ内

聯合軍總司令部民間情報係御中

Civil Information Division

G.H.Q 發 書

石井四郎軍醫中将に関する投書

勝ち抜く為だと長い間軍隊生活を強要せられ
着のみ着のまゝで復員してみれば 昨日に変る社会
の冷酷な扱ひ 家業は失はれ 然も昨今のインフレ
と就職難 資金を借りたくとも 借す人とてなく
十余名の家族を抱へての生活苦…これが生命を
さゝげて国家に奉仕して来た 私たちに與へられた
報酬の全部でした
終戦一ヶ年 凡ゆる努力を傾注して来ましたが
私たち一家の経済は愈々窮迫するばかり…此の
儘の状態で推移せんか 生活の破綻は
もう直き訪れるでせう

私は次第に生きる希望を失ひかけて参りました
私は時折 死の幻影にとりつかれます
何か刺戟があったら 或はそれに突進するでせう

かうした生活に陥入れたのは無謀な戦争を敢てした
軍国主義者に外なりません
日本は今民主的平和国家として生れ變らうとしてゐます
ほんとうに平和国家となる為には軍国主義信奉者は
完全に掃拭せられなければなりません 然し
終戦後の各内閣は 極力之が隠蔽と保護に
力を傾けてゐるのです
その一例は 既に召喚命令の出た 石井軍醫中将の

如き それで有ます　過日の新聞には 満洲よりの
一帰還者の談として 彼は満洲で 銃殺されたと
書いてゐました　それは 如何に 虚偽た 終始してゐる
ものであるか 私はよく知ってゐるのです
それは 政府の 指令に依る 宣傳以外の 何物でも
有ません
彼は 有名な 軍国主義者でした 典型的 国家主
義崇拝者でした　そして 又 人道の 敵でも 有ました
それが 故に 彼は 関東軍防疫給水部なるものを
創設したのでした　彼は 此處で 何をやったか
そして 何を 計画してゐたか
私は 彼の 部隊に 過去に 於て 勤務した事があった
のでよく 知ってゐるのです
石井四郎中将の 召喚に 依って その 内容は
白日下に 暴露されることは 國家主義者共の
如何に 虞れることか それが 故に 軍実を 隠蔽
秘匿して時です
彼の 召喚は A級戦犯者に 真に 不利な 事実を
提供致しませう 更に 皇族の 一員にさへも 累系
を及ぼすものなのです
それが 故に 終戦後 内閣就中 外務及び陸軍大臣
終戦連絡事務局 並に 復員廳は 弥更に 事
実を 闇に ほうむらうとしてゐるのです
悪德に みちた 彼等を 擁護し 及洞何筆の 罪の

ない 私たちが 犠牲にならねばならない こんな不合
理な事は有りません
彼の悪虐無道の行為を摘決し廣く輿論に
訴へ 彼と共に計画し或は関與した者たちの
罪悪は公正な神の裁きを受けしむることこそ
眞の平和國家建設の上から 其の前提とならね
ばなりません。
私は石井のこと、 彼が長たりし部隊の内容と
世期の惨虐行為の数々、構成分子等一切の
秘宓を知ってゐます
更に終戦如何になったか、 これも調査次第で
判明致しませう

若し御希望あれば 私は本件調査の為め得る
限りの御援助 御協力をしたいと思って居ります
私に若干の日子と 調査費用を御恵與下さるならば
必ず御期待に副ひ得る確信を有します
詳細に亘っては 御面談致し度存じます
若し亭ひに 調査の大役 お命じ下さるならば
本書到着 3日以内に 日本至済新聞紙上に
裏面の如き 出頭廣告御掲示方御願い
甲上げます　　　　　　　　　　　以上

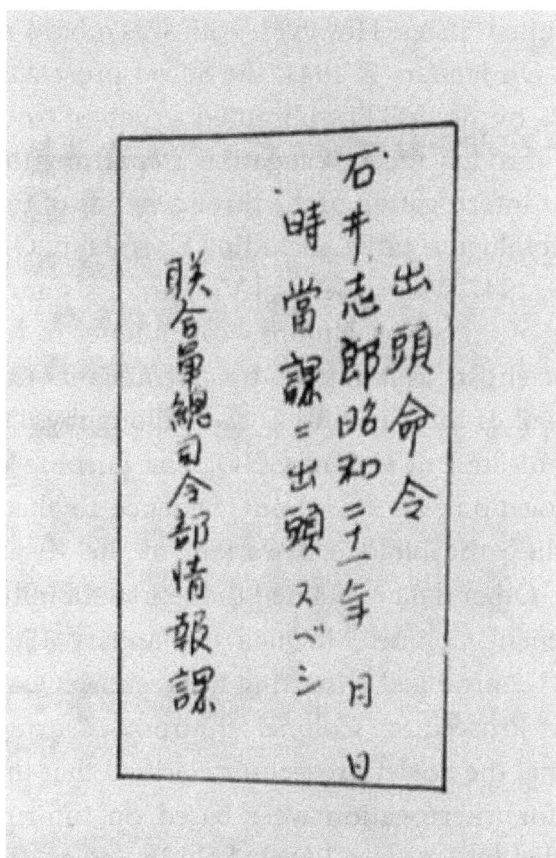

After GHQ filed the informant's letter, a new investigator, Sutton, arrived and Thompson returned to the United States. However, Ishii was a hard nut to crack. On January 7, 1947, the Soviet prosecutors of the IPS of the IMTFE submitted a request to G-2 of GHQ through the Investigation Department of the IPS for interrogation of the three generals of the Japanese biological units, including Shirō Ishii. On January 9, 1947, Major General Vasiliev, assistant prosecutor of the Soviet Union, wrote a letter to request the scientists submitted by Lieutenant Colonel McQuail of the GHQ, to C. A. Willoughby, Deputy Chief of Staff of G-2 of GHQ. The purpose of the interrogation was to submit evidence to the court regarding the biological warfare of the Kwantung Army. Other data contained the report submitted by Lieutenant Colonel McQuail on January 15, 1947, after G-2 arranged a meeting between McQuail and Soviet Prosecutor Colonel Smirnov. During the meeting, the Soviet prosecutor clarified that the reasons for interrogation were based on information provided by Japanese POWs held in Soviet custody, Kiyoshi Kawashima, leader of the Fourth Division of Unit 731, and his subordinate Tomio Karazawa. Lieutenant General Shirō Ishii, Colonel Kikuchi (leader of the First Division of Unit 731), and Colonel Ōta Sumi, the leader of the General Division of Unit 731, were suspected of crimes such as human experimentation, mass production of fleas and bacteria, methods of flea production, open air experiments at Anda and destruction of evidence at Ping Fan. The Soviet side stated that Japanese biological warfare technology was valuable not only to the Soviet Union but also to the United States. They proposed that when the three Japanese were interrogated, they should not be informed that they might become war criminals, and that they should swear not to reveal the interrogation to anyone.[47]

However, due to the United States wanting to claim moral superiority and claiming the research for national interests, they ignored the Soviet Union and sent more investigators to Tokyo. The United States then chose Dr. Norbert Fell, a civilian with a science background who was working at Fort Detrick, as the perfect man to run the investigation. Dr. Fell was Chief of the Planning Pilot-Engineering division at Camp Detrick. He arrived in Tokyo on April 16, 1947 and was able to obtain autopsy reports on anthrax and glanders as well as other dissertations from Unit 731 members.[48] It was Dr. Fell who enabled Dr. Naito to trade secrets in exchange for immunity. On May 1, 1947, Naito stated in an interrogation, "We want to cooperate and know we owe it to GHQ, but we have a responsibility to our

---

[47] National Archives of the United States, RG 331, B1434.
[48] National Archives of the United States, R319, E468, B428.

friends. We took an oath never to divulge information on human experiments. We are afraid some of us will be prosecuted as war criminals. We do not know how much others will be willing to give us. If you can give us documentary immunity, probably we can get everything. The subordinates, not the section chiefs, know the details. If we contact someone who is a Communist, he is liable to tell the Russians."[49] After the war, Dr. Naito became the founder of a successful pharmaceutical company, Green Cross. It wasn't until 1998 did Japanese historians realize that Dr. Naito had lied to American investigators in order to get out of trouble.

The Japanese scientists were aware of the relationship dynamic between the Soviet Union and the United States at the time and tried to leverage it. Ishii was especially good at that. At the time of his house arrest, the Soviet Union investigators arrived a couple of times in an attempt to interrogate him. Since the Americans were there, they became even more nervous about the potential for data on biological weapons leaking to the Soviet Union. According to Harumi later in her life, she remembered the American officers being nervous when Ishii's pet monkey was showing more familiarity with the American officers than with the Soviet Union.[50]

---

[49] Technical Library, Fort Dugway Proving Grounds, Utah, US.

[50] Hariss, Sheldon, *Factories of Death*, p. 213.

After Dr. Fell, Camp Detrick, of the United States army, sent two more researchers, Dr. Edwin V. Hill and Dr. Joseph Victor, to Japan to investigate. At that time, the tradeoff of conditions with Ishii and others in Japan regarding not being held responsible for war crimes had been established. The purpose of sending Hill and Victor to Japan was to further collect more information and verify the professional and technical data provided by Japan, including various reports and specimens of human experimentation.

In his summary report, Dr. Hill stated that the investigation was fully assisted by C. A. Willoughby, Deputy Chief of Staff of G-2 of the GHQ; moreover, those who were interrogated provided information voluntarily and did not request a guarantee of an exemption of their liabilities for war crimes during the interrogation. Willoughby was a key figure in the United States' decision-making process to "exempt" the Japanese biological warfare criminals from liability.[51]

In order to please the Soviet Union, the United States agreed to hand them a selected number of scientists for trial. Twelve scientists were selected to be sent to the Soviet Union for the Khabarovsk Trial. Due to the trial's remote location and the fact that the Soviet Union was a communist state, most of the

---

[51] National Archives of the United States, RG 331, B1434.

West saw the Khabarovsk trial as communist propaganda. However, the trial was actually very informative as the Soviet's style of interrogation was able to rattle the Japanese scientists into confessing.

Dr. Ishii Shiro, after all that he had created and done for the world, lived peacefully ever after. He died of throat cancer in 1959. Many of his subordinates became executives of pharmaceutical companies or held positions in the government.[52]

---

[52] Kristof, Nicholas D., "Unlocking a Deadly Secret", *New York Times*, 17 Mar 1995, p. 34-35.

Chapter 6

Modern Implication of Unit 731

Since the Japanese dumped cholera and typhoid cultures into the reservoirs, rivers and wells at the end of the war, it poisoned much of the water supply in China and caused countless Chinese deaths for years after the war ended. At the war's end, the Japanese also had released plague infested rats in Manchuria, causing another epidemic. "As the war ended, these rats caused outbreaks of the plague that killed at least 30,000 people in Harbin from 1946-1948."[53] An estimate of 700,000 to 2,000,000 chemical bombs were left in the region. Most had mustard gas and caused problems during the development of China in the 70s and 80s, and China became the largest chemical weapons cleanup area in the world.[54] There

---

[53] "The Other Holocaust: Nanjing Massacre, Unit 731, Unit 100, Unit 516," p. 5. Available from http://www.skycitygallery.com/japan/japan.html.
[54] Ibid., p. 9.

are tales of people in China who accidentally sat in a field in Harbin and ended up in the hospitals due to chemical weapons left behind during the war.

Camp Detrick had obtained the information from Ishii's Network and allegedly used the biological weapons developed by Unit 731 during the Korean War. In February of 1952, North Korea accused the United States of scattering bacteria causing insects near their military base. One could question the merits of these complaints. However, it is interesting to note that the epidemic hemorrhagic fever was not endemic to Korea before the Korean War and was a well-developed and researched topic of Unit 731.[55]

Many victims of germ warfare attacks which Ishii led suffered tremendously. In Zhejiang, where Ishii's unit had launched an attack, some of the victims suffered for more than 70 years. The local population discovered small black or red dots on their bodies, usually on their legs, a few days after the Japanese planes flew across town. As diseases developed, many died, but those who survived later developed rotten leg ailments. Nearly all the people with rotten leg ailments who are still alive were teenagers or even toddlers when they first developed the symptoms in the 1940s. Some developed rotten legs ailments after the 1940s while working in the fields.

---

[55] Gold, Hal, *Unit 731 Testimony*, p. 123-125.

The victims of germ warfare in China lived silently with their rotten leg disease for decades. Little was known even to the Japanese public until 1981 when the book "The Devil's Gluttony" was written by Seiichi Morimura. In 1997, court action was brought against the Japanese government seeking reparations for Chinese victims of Japanese germ warfare. On August 11, 1997, 180 plaintiffs who were victims of the biological attacks sought compensation for the damage that had been inflicted upon them. The Tokyo court confirmed that Unit 731 did conduct germ warfare in China killing many and causing injuries from bubonic plague, typhoid, and other related diseases. However, the Japanese government continues to deny that its Army ever used biological agents in China.[56]

Finally, in 2014, there were programs at several hospitals in Shanghai to provide effective treatment for the victims including wound cleaning and a series of skin grafts which otherwise could have been prohibitively costly. After more than 70 years of suffering, some of the victims finally could wear socks and shoes to visit their relatives and take life changing steps.[57]

---

[56] "Damages Sought by Victims of Biological Warfare in China," *The Japan Times*, Aug 11, 1997, https://www.japantimes.co.jp/news/1997/08/11/national/damages-sought-by-victims-of-biological-warfare-in-china/.

[57] "Meet Wang Xuan, China", Nobel Women Initiative, https://nobelwomensinitiative.org/meet-wang-xuan-china/.

Justice was never properly received by those who suffered from the biological weapons program. Ishii's genius could have been spent elsewhere if he had been born at a different time. His work could have created an immense difference in terms of world affairs. If the information Ishii had supplied was of so little value that government officials downplayed it, the United States might have presented him for trial in the Soviet Union. Since the United States acquired information for itself, many of the weapons America subsequently has used are a product of Ishii's Network's research in one form or another. Yet, most Westerners have neither heard of Dr. Ishii Shiro nor of Unit 731.

OTHER RELATED BOOKS

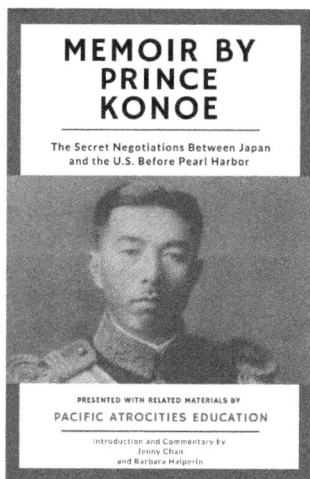

MEMOIR BY PRINCE KONOE

The Secret Negotiations Between Japan
and the U.S. Before Pearl Harbor

PRESENTED WITH RELATED MATERIALS BY
PACIFIC ATROCITIES EDUCATION

Introduction and Commentary by
Jenny Chan
and Barbara Halperin

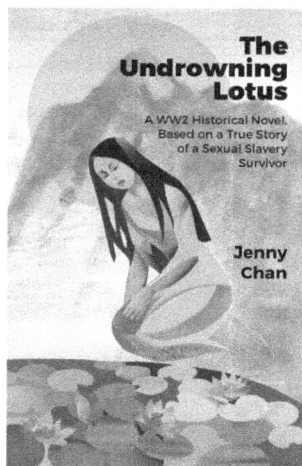

The Undrowning Lotus

A WW2 Historical Novel,
Based on a True Story
of a Sexual Slavery
Survivor

Jenny
Chan

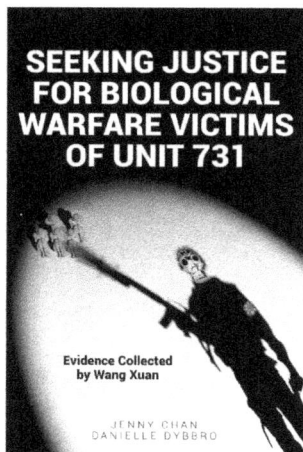

SEEKING JUSTICE FOR BIOLOGICAL WARFARE VICTIMS OF UNIT 731

Evidence Collected
by Wang Xuan

JENNY CHAN
DANIELLE DYBBRO

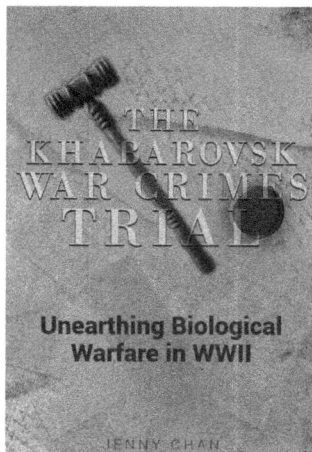

THE KHABAROVSK WAR CRIMES TRIAL

Unearthing Biological
Warfare in WWII

JENNY CHAN

www.ingramcontent.com/pod-product-compliance
Lightning Source LLC
Chambersburg PA
CBHW060344050426
42449CB00011B/2817